A Brief Guide
to
Georgia Evictions

Second Edition

by Michael R. Dunham

Copyright (c) 2012, 2016. All rights reserved.

"My work as a trial judge presiding over landlord and tenant cases in Fulton County, Georgia since 1984, and that of my colleagues everywhere in this State, would have been easier if all landlords appearing in our Courts were required to read this book. Mr. Dunham's book is a "must read" for any landlord, whether a lawyer or pro se litigant, who wants to navigate effectively before and during the eviction process."

- Hon. Louis Levenson

Contents

Appendices

Introduction

I wrote this book because it needed to be written. I intend for this book to serve primarily as a valuable resource for the non-lawyer who owns or manages rental property in Georgia and needs a practical guide to the eviction process in Georgia. However, this book will also assist the practicing attorney who has no significant experience with Georgia landlord-tenant law. The goal of this book is to familiarize the reader with the process in Georgia by which a tenant is removed from rental property legally, but involuntarily.

I also want to stress what this book is not. Although citations to Georgia law are included for reference where appropriate, this book is not, and was never intended to be, a comprehensive treatise on Georgia landlord-tenant law. A reader looking for such a treatise would be well-advised to review a copy of *Dawkins, Ga. Landlord and Tenant – Breach and Remedies (with forms)*, which is in its fourth edition as of this writing. If I have done my job, however, this book will serve as a companion and complement to Mr. Dawkins's excellent work.

I am qualified to write this book because of my own experience, not because of academic expertise. I have practiced law in Georgia for more than a decade. I have litigated countless cases in the landlord-tenant arena. I have represented both landlords and tenants, in both residential and commercial contexts. I have also served as a mediator in the Fulton County Landlord-Tenant

Mediation Program (connected with the Magistrate Court of that county), where I heard some 200 cases as a mediator in the span of less than a year. I do not intend the insights offered in this book to be scholarly advice; rather, the reader should view them first and foremost as pragmatic suggestions from a practitioner "in the trenches."

This book roughly tracks the eviction process which the landlord should follow, beginning with pre-suit considerations; proceeding through the drafting and filing of the claim; ensuring the tenant is properly served; trying the case in court; and then handling any appeal issues. I have also included a chapter explaining alternative dispute resolution ("ADR"), the popularity of which is increasing every year. Along the way, should the reader encounter a term with which he is not familiar, I have included a brief glossary at the end of the book.

There are also a couple of new additions in the second edition of this book. There is a paragraph at the end of chapter 2 explaining the applicability of the federal Servicemembers Civil Relief Act [50 U.S.C. §§ 501 et seq.] and how the landlord can avoid certain traps for the unwary. There is a paragraph at the end of chapter 3 explaining what the "covenant of quiet enjoyment" is and how a tenant could exploit it as a defense. I have also included two new appendices, explaining quiet enjoyment and the landlord's obligation to maintain the premises in greater detail, as well as explaining the proper handling of security deposits.

I have also highlighted a number of "practice pointers" for the reader's benefit throughout the book. Generally speaking, these "practice pointers" represent pragmatic considerations and practices I have recommended based on my experience. A summary of all of the "practice pointers" highlighted throughout the main text is included in Appendix E.

As with any legal problem, a landlord reading this book intending to represent himself should consider seeking the advice of a licensed attorney competent in the area of Georgia landlord-tenant law. Nothing in this book is intended as, or should be construed as, legal advice to the reader.

A note on pronouns – centuries of use have effectively neutered the male pronoun in formal writing. I have exclusively used male pronouns ("he," "his," "him") throughout this book. This is not to suggest the referenced parties cannot be females or entities, and the reader should read (for instance) "he" as "he, she, or it" wherever appropriate. In addition, all references to the singular should be construed as inclusive of the plural, and vice versa, wherever appropriate.

I hope you find the materials in this book useful. If you have questions, comments, suggestions, or even (constructive) criticism, please feel free to contact me at the web site below.

Thank you, and good luck!

– Michael R. Dunham
www.GeorgiaEvictionBook.com

Eviction in Georgia is a legal process, with certain carefully defined steps and procedures. Before resorting to that process, however, the threshold question is whether it can be avoided entirely. Generally speaking, although landlords in Georgia enjoy considerable rights and advantages when it comes time to dispossess a tenant who is in violation of his lease, it will rarely be the case that "self-help" eviction is legally appropriate.

A landlord who attempts to evict a tenant without using the judicial process puts himself at considerable risk, as the landlord will face potential liability for wrongful eviction, that is, where a landlord unlawfully and intentionally interferes with a tenant's right of possession arising under a valid lease. Wrongful eviction is an intentional tort in Georgia, and if successful, the tenant may be entitled to claim punitive damages in addition to other available forms of tort damages.[1] Other remedies potentially available to tenants for wrongful eviction include specific performance of the lease agreement.[2] Alternatively, the tenant may seek a declaratory judgment relating to his rights under the lease agreement.[3] For example, in one case,[4] an apartment complex evicted its tenant's adult brother from the tenant's apartment on the basis that the brother was not listed on the lease, and the tenant (who had otherwise occupied the apartment pursuant to a valid lease to which she was a party) sued the complex for wrongful eviction. The Court of Appeals found the fact the tenant may have been in violation of her lease did not prevent a potential recovery for wrongful eviction.

To lawfully dispossess a tenant who is in violation of his lease, the landlord is typically required to follow the statutory procedure outlined in the Georgia Code.[5] However, in the context of a commercial lease, it is possible to waive the statutory dispossessory process by advance agreement, usually by including a provision in the lease to accomplish this specific goal.[6] Nonetheless, the landlord should be very cautious about carrying out a "self-help" eviction, even with the protection of a properly drafted contractual provision allowing such a remedy, as any breach of the peace will potentially give rise to a claim for wrongful eviction, as will the landlord's own violation of the lease agreement.[7] Note, however, it is not possible to waive the statutory dispossessory process in a residential lease. Any contractual provision which attempts to waive the tenant's access to the courts is unenforceable under Georgia law, as a matter of public policy affording due process to residential tenants, who may be relatively unsophisticated in the art of negotiating lease agreements.

Notwithstanding the above, a landlord is entitled to reenter the premises if they have been abandoned by the tenant. A careful draftsman will include a provision in the lease agreement allowing the landlord to reenter the premises upon abandonment for the purpose of reletting the same as the agent for the abandoning tenant, as well as for the purpose of securing and protecting the premises. If the tenant has left personal property behind, and the landlord is able to determine that said property has also been abandoned, then the landlord may remove that property without resorting to the statutory dispossessory process.[8] Of course, whether a tenant has actually "abandoned" property or the rented premises can be difficult to determine under some circumstances, and an inquiry into the specific facts of the case will be necessary. If the landlord has any doubt, the dispossessory process should be followed.

> **Practice Pointer #1: If possible, the landlord should be sure to include a provision in the lease agreement allowing him to reenter the premises upon abandonment for the purpose of reletting the same as the agent for the abandoning tenant, as well as for the purpose of securing and protecting the premises.**

> **Practice Pointer #2: If there is any doubt, the landlord should follow the dispossessory process.**

---

[1] Albert Properties, Inc. v. Watkins, 143 Ga. App. 184 (1977).

[2] Peachtree on Peachtree Investors, Ltd. v. Reed Drug Co., 251 Ga. 692 (1983).

[3] General Hosp. v. Jenkins, 188 Ga. App. 825 (1988).

[4] Kerlin v. Lane Co., 165 Ga. App. 622 (1983).

[5] O.C.G.A. §§ 44-7-50 et seq. See Chapter 2.

[6] Colonial Self Storage of the South East, Inc. v. Concord Properties, Inc., 147 Ga. App. 493 (1978).

[7] Swift Loan & Finance Co., Inc. v. Duncan, 195 Ga. App. 556 (1990).

[8] Spitzer v. Selig Enterprises, Inc., 140 Ga. App. 156 (1976).

Once the landlord determines it is necessary to resort to the judicial system to regain possession of the rented premises, Georgia law actually puts two different statutory remedies at the landlord's disposal – a dispossessory action, and a distress action, which are not necessarily exclusive. There is also a third possibility, that is, a conventional suit for breach of contract.

Dispossessory Action. In virtually all cases, the landlord will want to file a standard dispossessory action. The procedures for a dispossessory action are set forth in the Georgia Code at O.C.G.A. §§ 44-7-50 et seq.[9] Generally, the landlord will file such an action in the Magistrate Court of the county in which the rented premises are located. The Magistrate Court is a court of limited jurisdiction, and it is commonly referred to as "small claims" court. Ordinarily, the jurisdictional limit (i.e., the maximum amount of money which can be recovered in the form of a judgment) in Magistrate Court is $15,000.00, but this jurisdictional limit does not apply to money judgments for rent issued in dispossessory cases.[10] In other words, a landlord may sue for more than $15,000.00 in past due rent and other damages in a dispossessory action, if appropriate.

There are several reasons why one might consider filing the dispossessory action in Superior Court (or possibly State Court, if one exists in the jurisdiction where the case will be filed – see the endnote for a brief explanation of the differences between the two).[11] First, if the landlord wishes to seek a form of relief other than a money judgment and a writ of possession (e.g., any form of equitable relief such as an injunction), then the case should be filed in Superior Court. Second, discovery devices available under the Georgia Civil Practice Act – such as interrogatories, requests for admission, requests for production of documents, and depositions – are not available in the Magistrate Court (although the Magistrate Court can enter an order allowing the use of such procedures at its discretion). Third, the losing party in a Magistrate Court action has a right to a appeal to a court of record in that county for a trial de novo. A trial de novo means the second court will start from "square one" when it hears the case, rather than starting from the record from which the appeal was taken, effectively giving the tenant a "second bite at the apple" in the form of a retrial of his case. Filing initially in the Superior or State Court would therefore remove the need to try the case twice. In practice, however, time and expense will typically overwhelm these concerns, as the landlord will want to move the case through the court system as quickly and cheaply as possible – a feat which is almost always more easily accomplished in Magistrate Court.

If the landlord is an entity rather than a natural person, there is potentially one major advantage to filing in Magistrate Court as opposed to a Superior or State Court. Although under Georgia law natural persons have a constitutional right to represent themselves in lawsuits, the Georgia Supreme Court has held that this right does not extend to an entity, which must be represented by a licensed attorney. However, this requirement only applies in courts of record (i.e., Superior Court or State Court), and since Magistrate Court is not a court of record, an entity may be represented in magistrate court by an "agent" who is not an attorney (e.g., a principal of the entity, a property manager, etc.).[12]

Practice Pointer #3: Generally speaking, the landlord should file and prosecute dispossessory actions in Magistrate Court, where the case will generally

move more quickly and cheaply, and where it is possible in most cases for the landlord to proceed without hiring counsel.

Distraint Proceeding. In addition to the dispossessory proceeding, the other form of relief offered under Georgia law is known as a distress proceeding or a distraint proceeding. The procedures for a distraint proceeding are set forth in the Georgia Code at O.C.G.A. §§ 44-7-70 et seq.[13] A landlord has a general lien on most personal property belonging to the tenant,[14] and distraint is the summary procedure by which the landlord may foreclose upon that lien. However, since the tenant is afforded both notice of and a hearing in the distraint proceeding before losing possession of his property, the practical utility of a distraint proceeding is slight. Until the hearing, the landlord is not allowed to secure the premises against removal of the property. Hence, the tenant can simply remove his property from the rented premises before the hearing, which obviously compromises the functionality of the distraint procedure. In addition, if the landlord loses the distraint action, he is potentially liable to the tenant for whatever foreseeable damages might arise from his wrongful conduct.[15]

As a practical matter, a distraint proceeding is generally only worthwhile in a situation where the tenant has abandoned significant property on the premises under circumstances where the landlord has an independent right to enter and secure the premises (i.e., the lease agreement provides for the landlord to have that right). It is perfectly legal to file both a distraint proceeding and a dispossessory proceeding against the same tenant and to have both actions pending at the same time, and in a typical case where the landlord wishes to file a distraint proceeding, it is highly advisable that a dispossessory proceeding is also simultaneously filed. The two cases can be filed in the same court and can typically be consolidated for trial, although the consent of both parties is required to consolidate (assuming the tenant has filed an answer in both cases).

7

> **Practice Pointer #4: The landlord should generally only consider filing a distraint proceeding if the tenant has abandoned property of significant value on the premises under circumstances where the landlord has an independent right to enter and secure the premises.**

Conventional Lawsuit. Of course, a third possible course of action would be to forego the filing of a dispossessory action entirely, in favor of a more traditional lawsuit for breach of contract. The object of a dispossessory action is to recover possession of the rented premises for the landlord – an action that has the collateral effect of terminating the lease agreement, including the obligation of the tenant for future rental payments. It may be the case that the landlord is willing to allow the tenant to remain in possession of the premises, and to allow future rental payments to continue to accrue, resorting to a more conventional lawsuit as a means of liquidating the damages flowing from the tenant's breach of his obligation to pay rent. In addition, a suit for rent may be required if the tenant has already vacated the rented premises, since it may not be possible to perfect personal service on the tenant in a dispossessory action, which would mean the court adjudicating the dispossessory action would not have jurisdiction to enter a money judgment against the tenant.[16]

Servicemembers Civil Relief Act [50 U.S.C. §§ 501 et seq.]. The Servicemembers Civil Relief Act ("SCRA") is a federal law designed to protect soldiers and sailors from suffering adverse results in court during their military service. The landlord should be very careful before dispossessing a soldier, as proceeding with an eviction may actually be a federal crime under the SCRA.

In general, the landlord cannot evict a servicemember or his dependents (defined as the servicemember's spouse, children, and anyone for whom he has provided more than half of the dependent's support over the preceding 180 days) from a residential property where the rent is less than a certain amount,[17] unless the landlord first obtains a court order. As a practical matter, this means the landlord must follow the dispossessory process and apply for a writ of possession. However, if the servicemember has the ability to pay the rent, the Court may stay an eviction proceeding for 90 days (or more or less, if the interests of justice so require, as determined by the Court), and if the servicemember asks for the stay,[18] the Court is required to grant such a stay. Of course, the servicemember must still ensure the rent is paid in the meantime, and the SCRA provides a mechanism whereby the rent can be automatically deducted from the servicemember's pay and paid directly to the landlord.[19]

The SCRA also provides for a tenant to be able to terminate a lease early if he enters military service or is active-duty military and is deployed elsewhere.[20] There are notice requirements with which the servicemember must comply,[21] but if proper notice is given, the lease will generally be terminated thirty (30) days after the first date after delivery of the notice on which the next rental payment is due and payable pursuant to the lease agreement.[22] The servicemember continues to be responsible for payment of all rent and other obligations arising under the lease which are due on or before the date the lease is deemed terminated, although the landlord may not impose an early termination charge.[23]

---

[9] See Appendix A.

[10] Atlanta J's, Inc. v. Houston Foods, Inc., 237 Ga. App. 415 (1999).

[11] While every county has a Superior Court, which is a trial court of general jurisdiction, only larger counties have a State Court. Both are courts of record (as opposed to the Magistrate Court, which is not a court of record). The primary difference between the Superior Court and the State Court is that equitable remedies are only available in the Superior Court. As a practical matter, in the dispossessory context, this is a distinction without

a difference.

[12] Eckles v. Atlanta Technology Group, Inc., 267 Ga. 801 (1997).

[13] See Appendix A.

[14] O.C.G.A. § 44-14-341.

[15] O.C.G.A. § 44-7-77(b).

[16] See Chapter 6.

[17] The SCRA provides for protection where the monthly rent "does not exceed $2,400" as of 2003, but the SCRA also provides for that amount to be adjusted annually based on the Consumer Price Index. As of 2015, the maximum monthly rent to which the SCRA applied is $3,329.84. The Secretary of Defense is responsible for publishing the new amount every year. See 50 U.S.C. App. § 531(a)(2).

[18] 50 U.S.C. App. § 531(b).

[19] 50 U.S.C. App. § 531(d).

[20] 50 U.S.C. App. § 535.

[21] 50 U.S.C. App. § 535(c)(1)(A), (c)(2).

[22] 50 U.S.C. App. § 535(d)(1). Note if the lease provides for something other than monthly rent (e.g., week-to-week), then the lease terminates on the last day of the month after the month in which the lease termination notice was delivered.

[23] 50 U.S.C. App. § 535(e)(1).

Assuming the landlord has determined it is necessary to file a dispossessory action, there are several steps which must be taken first. These steps should not, and in most cases cannot, be skipped, at the risk of the litigation itself failing.

Required Basis for Dispossession. There are three grounds for dispossession described in the Georgia Code.[24] The first is that the tenant is a "hold-over" tenant, that is, he continues to hold possession of the premises over and beyond the term for which they were rented or leased. The second (and, in practice, most commonly asserted) is that the tenant has failed to pay his rent when due. The third is that the tenant is a tenant at will or a tenant at sufferance,[25] and the owner wishes to recover possession. These are alternative grounds, meaning only one of them must exist in order for the landlord to be able to maintain a dispossessory action. However, if none of the three statutory grounds is alleged or proved, then the landlord cannot maintain the dispossessory action.

Demand for Possession. In all cases, the statute requires that a demand for possession must be made before filing a dispossessory action, as a condition precedent to filing the same. A demand for possession made before trial but after the commencement of the dispossessory action is legally insufficient; the demand must be made before the case is filed.[26] There is no "magic language" or particular form required for a demand for possession to be effective, so long as the demand is clear and unequivocal,[27] but as a practical matter it is far easier to prove a written demand than an oral demand.

How the notice is sent will usually be a function of how much the landlord is willing to spend and how quickly the return will be needed. Traditionally, it was considered good practice in most cases to send a written demand for possession by both certified mail and regular mail. However, in practice, certified mail may be slower and/or less reliable than necessary to be sure the landlord has proof of receipt by the time of trial. An overnight (or second-day or third-day) delivery service such as FedEx Express or UPS may be preferable, although these services will be more expensive. Another alternative might be to use a third party (either a trusted friend or a professional courier service) to hand-deliver the notice, but this tends to be very expensive, and the delivery person will have to be available to testify at trial. In addition to the above considerations, if the lease prescribes a particular form or procedure for the demand for possession or for notices to the tenant in general, then compliance with these provisions of the lease is required.

> **Practice Pointer #5: The landlord should consider methods of delivering the written demand for possession other than regular or certified mail, to ensure he can prove delivery of the demand for possession later.**

There are three things to keep in mind regarding the demand for possession. First, a demand for possession is not the same as (and, standing alone, does not necessarily accomplish) a termination of the lease agreement, and it is not necessary that the demand for possession also terminate the lease agreement, although one could accomplish both objectives in the same letter.[28] Second, once a demand for possession is made, the landlord should be careful about taking subsequent actions which are inconsistent with that demand, or else the landlord could be deemed to have waived the demand. If such actions are taken (such as accepting rent after the demand for possession, even if rent is past due – see below), then a new demand for possession should be made before a dispossessory action is filed. Finally, there is a limited exception to the demand requirement which exists in a case where the landlord can prove such a demand would be futile. In practice, however, the landlord is well-advised to make a demand for possession in all cases, rather than hoping to be able to prove futility at a later time.

Practice Pointer #6: The landlord should always make a written demand for possession, and he should thereafter behave as if he wants the tenant to vacate the premises.

Additional Step for Termination of Tenancy at Will. In an action to dispossess a tenant for holding over and/or for failing to timely pay rent, there are no additional conditions precedent to filing suit. However, in an action to dispossess a tenant at will (defined as a tenant whose tenancy has no specified time of termination),[29] the landlord must also terminate the tenancy, which requires a notice of at least sixty (60) days. (Note this sixty-day notice is not required to terminate a tenancy at sufferance, which arises where the tenant comes into lawful possession of the premises initially, but wrongfully remains in possession after the expiration of his lawful right, without the landlord's permission.) If the tenant continues to hold over beyond the period described in the termination notice, then the landlord should make a demand for possession. As previously noted, it is possible (though not required) to terminate the tenancy and demand possession effective at the end of the notice period in the same instrument.

Insistence on Strict Performance. If the landlord intends to dis-possess a tenant for failing to pay rent when due, the landlord should first review the tenant's payment history vis-à-vis the requirements of the lease. If the landlord has accepted late pay-ments from the tenant in the past, then the landlord could be found to have waived his right to insist upon timely payment.[30] However, the landlord can reinstate this right by giving written notice to the tenant that late payments will no longer be accept-ed. In this situation, the landlord should also demand payment of whatever past-due rent has accrued before filing a dispposses-sory action for failure to pay rent.

Refusal of Post-Demand Rent Payments. In addition to the fore-going actions which the landlord may be required to take, if the landlord intends to dispossess a tenant for failing to pay rent when due, the landlord *must not accept rent payments in any amount* after the demand for possession is made. Acceptance of such a payment – even if less than the total amount due – will effectively waive the landlord's right to dispossess the ten-ant, and in some situations could give the tenant the ability to plead the defense of accord and satisfaction when a claim for rent is filed.[31] Thus, while the landlord's desire to obtain at least a partial payment from the tenant may be understandable, if the landlord wishes to recover possession of the premises, the proper action for the landlord to take upon tender by the tenant is to promptly refuse or return the same.

> **Practice Pointer #7: The landlord who wishes to evict a tenant for failing to pay rent must not accept rent payments in any amount after making a demand for possession.**

However, if the dispossessory action has been filed and served and the parties are awaiting trial, the landlord may suggest that the tenant pay his rent into the registry of the court pending the outcome of the case, which would give the landlord an avenue of collection if he ultimately prevails at trial. If the issue of possession is contested and cannot be determined within two weeks after the tenant is served with the dispossessory action then the tenant is required by law to deposit rent and utility payments required by the lease into the registry of the court.[32]

In addition, in a dispossessory action filed solely for nonpayment of rent, if the tenant tenders payment within seven days after service of process, he may tender payment of the amount claimed as past-due rent, plus the costs of the dispossessory action, and the landlord is bound to accept the same. If this is done, the tenant shall have a complete defense to the dispossessory action. The tenant can only take advantage of this statutory defense one time in any given twelve-month period, however.[33]

---

[24] O.C.G.A. § 44-7-50(a).

[25] A "tenant at will" arises where the landlord and tenant have not included a provision in their lease terminating the tenancy at a particular time. A "tenant at sufferance" is a tenant who lawfully came into possession, but wrongfully remains in possession.

[26] Terrell v. Griffith, 129 Ga. App. 675 (1973).

[27] Stephens v. Housing Authority, 163 Ga. App. 97 (1982).

[28] O.C.G.A. § 44-7-50(b). Note there is an exception to this rule if the landlord is a public housing authority.

[29] O.C.G.A. § 44-7-6.

[30] Oastler v. Wright, 201 Ga. 649 (1946).

[31] Gay v. American Oil Co., 115 Ga. App. 18 (1967); Rafizadeh v. KR Snellville, LLC, 280 Ga. App. 613 (2006).

[32] O.C.G.A. § 44-7-54(a).

[33] O.C.G.A. § 44-7-52(a).

Once the landlord has elected to sue and has taken all of the presuit steps necessary, the next step is to prepare the filing that will initiate the lawsuit. Due care in the preparation of the initial filing can ultimately make the landlord's job much easier at trial.

Requirements of Complaint. Ordinarily, a lawsuit is commenced when the plaintiff files a pleading known as a complaint. The dispossessory statute technically requires the landlord's "affidavit under oath to the facts," not a complaint, although a complaint verified by the landlord is the functional equivalent and would presumably be sufficient. The landlord's affidavit should specifically state the statutory ground(s) upon which the dispossessory action is to be based, that is, that the tenant is holding over,[34] has failed to pay rent when due, or is a tenant at will or at sufferance.[35] If the action is based on more than one of the statutory grounds, then it should state them all, pled in the alternative.[36] The landlord's affidavit must also specifically state that demand for possession has been made and the tenant has refused the same. Finally, the landlord's affidavit should set forth a comprehensive prayer for relief, which includes requests for a writ of possession as well as a money judgment for past-due rent, rent accruing up to the date of judgment or vacancy at a specified rate, accrued interest, and/or attorney's fees, if applicable and allowed (or at least, not forbidden) by the lease.

Exhibits. It is not required that the lease, the demand for possession, or any other evidence must be attached to or filed with the landlord's affidavit. However, including and incorporating as much documentary evidence as possible in this initial filing is strongly recommended. This is because in practice the evidence "admitted" during the trial of the case – particularly in Magistrate Court, where most dispossessory actions are filed and prosecuted – is often not actually filed in the record, but rather is returned to the parties at the conclusion of the trial. If the case is subsequently appealed, the record which is transferred to the State or Superior Court is actually not complete, since the trial exhibits are not included. Including this evidence in the record from the beginning of the case cures that problem, and can potentially enable the court to act without the need for a hearing in certain circumstances, particularly while the case is on appeal or if the case is transferred before trial. Moreover, if the documents are incorporated into the initial filing – which, as noted, is essentially a verified complaint, since the landlord's affidavit is given "under oath" – and the tenant fails to dispute the same, the landlord may argue that the tenant may not dispute the documents at trial.[37]

> **Practice Pointer #8: The landlord should attach copies of the lease agreement, demand for possession, and any other relevant documents as exhibits to the initial affidavit.**

Summons. The summons is a standard document, similar in form to the summons required in most other civil cases. The major difference between the summons in a general civil case and the summons in a dispossessory action is that the latter should specify the answer is due seven (7) days after service, not thirty (30) days as is typical in other cases. In practice, many jurisdictions (particularly State and Magistrate Courts in larger counties) have created their own form, which generally incorporates the summons and landlord's affidavit into the same instrument. If the jurisdiction where the dispossessory action will be filed has its own form, the landlord should use that form, in order to speed processing of his case and minimize the potential for errors in handling the same. The attachment of additional documents, including an additional statement of facts or prayers for relief, to the court's standard form is almost certain to be permitted, if the need arises.

Practice Pointer #9: The landlord should use the Court's own form whenever possible.

Service of Process. The dispossessory statute ostensibly requires personal service upon the tenant(s).[38] However, the statute specifically authorizes service to be perfected upon "any person who is sui juris[39] residing on the premises." Alternatively, if no one is found to be residing in the premises, service may be perfected by posting a copy of the summons and landlord's affidavit on the door of the rented premises and mailing a copy of the same to the tenant's last known address (commonly referred to as "tack-and-mail" or "nail-and-mail" service). It should be noted, however, if personal service is not perfected, the trial court only has jurisdiction to award a writ of possession, and the trial court may not award a money judgment against the tenant.[40] In other words, personal service is required if the landlord wishes to recover anything other than a writ of possession, such as a money judgment for past due rent or attorney's fees.

Practice Pointer #10: If the landlord wishes to recover a money judgment against the tenant, the landlord must ensure the tenant is personally served with process in the dispossessory action, and the landlord should consider using a specially appointed process server, if appropriate.

[34] A tenant is "holding over" when he continues to occupy the rented premises beyond the end of the rental term.

[35] A "tenant at will" arises where the landlord and tenant have not included a provision in their lease terminating the tenancy at a particular time. A "tenant at sufferance" is a tenant who lawfully came into possession, but wrongfully remains in possession.

[36] Pleading "in the alternative" simply means the landlord is alleging (for instance) that the tenant should be dispossessed because he is holding over the premises beyond the rented term, and/or because he has failed to pay the rent when due. In other words, both grounds can be alleged, but only one must be proven for the landlord to win the case.

[37] See Appendix D.

[38] O.C.G.A. § 44-7-51(a).

[39] A mentally competent adult is generally sui juris, as are teenagers in most instances.

[40] O.C.G.A. § 44-7-51(c).

Now that the landlord has filed suit, the only way to win the case (absent some sort of settlement) is to effectively try the case in such a manner that the trial court can be convinced to award the landlord that which he seeks. The landlord should be prepared to spend considerable time preparing for trial, if he is to assure himself the greatest chance of victory.

It is not uncommon, particularly in a larger county, for a one-day dispossessory calendar to have dozens or even hundreds of cases set for trial that day. Many of these cases will likely result in dismissals or default judgments, but the court will still be required to hear evidence to support any money judgment which may be sought. Given the considerable strain which such a voluminous calendar will put on the trial judge and court personnel, preparation for trial should be done with the efficient use of the court's time foremost in mind

General Considerations When Preparing for Trial. As in any other civil trial, the normal rules of evidence apply, as do the civil practice rules applicable in the court in which the case is filed.[41] As is typical in any civil case, hearsay (a statement made by someone other than the witness) is generally inadmissible to prove the landlord's case. Thus one or more witnesses competent to testify about the relevant evidence should be present. If the landlord will have witnesses testify, it would be prudent to issue valid subpoenas (available from the clerk of court for a nominal fee) to secure the witnesses' attendance, even if the witnesses are "friendly," to enable the landlord to seek a continuance if a necessary witness is for some reason unable to attend the trial. Although in practice many evidentiary and other technicalities are often dispensed with in Magistrate Court and/ or where one or both parties are *pro se*, the parties and their lawyers should treat the trial of a dispossessory action with the same level of dignity, care, and attention to detail as any other civil action, and to prepare accordingly. However, any allegation in the landlord's affidavit which the tenant does not deny may be deemed admitted for the purposes of the trial.

Practice Pointer #11: The landlord should obtain and serve subpoenas on each of his trial witnesses, even if they are "friendly" witnesses.

Evidentiary Requirements. The landlord bears the burden of proving his claims by a preponderance of the evidence, meaning the evidence is such that the Court finds it is more likely than not that the landlord's claims are true. To accomplish this goal, the landlord should be prepared to present whatever testimony and/or documentary evidence is necessary to make out his claims. At a minimum, this will generally include copies of the lease agreement (or the original, if available) and any correspondence between the parties, especially the demand for possession. This is true even if the tenant has not filed an answer, even though this failure by the tenant has the legal effect of admitting the facts alleged in the dispossessory affidavit. If the tenant has filed an answer, careful thought should be given to whatever defenses the tenant asserted in his answer or which the tenant might assert at trial. If the tenant has asserted a counterclaim, the landlord should carefully consider whatever defenses he might have to the counterclaim. Although under Georgia law the landlord is not required to specifically answer the counterclaims via a separate pleading, and bearing in mind the tenant will bear the same burden of proof on the counterclaim that the landlord must bear on his main claims, the landlord must nevertheless be prepared to resist the tenant's counterclaim at trial and should not take for granted that the Court will deny them if the landlord does not resist.[42]

There are two common examples of documents that the landlord should present but will often forget. If the ground for the dispossession is a failure to pay rent, and the tenant has attempted to pay rent but the landlord has refused, the landlord will hopefully have had the foresight to memorialize the refusal of the rent in a written communication to the tenant, and this document should be made available for trial. If a money judgment for rent or other charges is sought, the landlord would be wise to prepare a summary of how the amount demanded is calculated, which should also be introduced as an exhibit at trial (with the proper foundation, of course). In a similar vein, the landlord should be ready and able to present a complete payment history for the tenant if possible. This may be especially important if there is a dispute over when and how much was paid, particularly if the landlord has ever accepted irregular or partial payments from the tenant.

Practice Pointer #12: If the landlord has refused an attempted tender of rent by the tenant, the landlord should write a follow-up letter or other communication memorializing that refusal and the reasons therefor, and copies of that communication should be available to be used as an exhibit at trial.

Practice Pointer #13: If the landlord desires a money judgment for any reason, and the total amount requested must be calculated somehow, the landlord should prepare a written summary of those calculations and be prepared to admit that written summary as an exhibit at trial.

The landlord should bring at least three copies of any document which he expects to introduce at trial – one for the court, one for the tenant, and one for himself. If the document is to be admitted through the testimony of a witness other than the landlord or the tenant, the landlord should consider a fourth copy of the exhibit, for the witness to reference directly. To save time at trial, the landlord should give a copy of all documents which he expects to introduce into evidence to the tenant before the case is actually called for trial. There is little advantage, if any, to be gained from withholding documents from the tenant in this situation, and whatever slight advantage the landlord might perceive will be more than outweighed by the annoyance which the trial court will have at the landlord's failure to extend this basic litigation courtesy. If the case is referred to pretrial mediation, documents should be exchanged in mediation even if the case does not settle.

> **Practice Pointer #14: The landlord should share all of his trial exhibits with the tenant at his earliest opportunity, to save time at trial.**

Note the need for thorough preparation is not necessarily obviated by the tenant's failure to timely file an answer, unless the landlord seeks nothing more than a writ of possession. If the landlord seeks a money judgment and has obtained personal service on the tenant, then the landlord will have to be prepared to present evidence supporting his claim for damages.

Sometimes, cases must be continued for some reason or another (e.g., one of the parties, or a witness under subpoena, falls ill or is otherwise unavoidably unable to attend the trial). If that happens, the court may continue the case to another trial calendar. If the trial will not take place within two weeks after service of the landlord's affidavit is perfected, the court must require the payment of rent into the court's registry.[43] The landlord should be sure to remind the court of this legal requirement, to ensure such a provision is included in the order resetting the case.

Practice Pointer #15: The landlord should be prepared to tactfully remind the Court that if the trial must be continued to a date more than two weeks after the tenant was served with the landlord's affidavit, the Court must require the payment of rent into the Court's registry.

---

[41] In Superior Court or State Court, the applicable procedural rules are found in the Civil Practice Act, O.C.G.A. §§ 9-11-1 et seq. In Magistrate Court, the applicable procedural rules are found at O.C.G.A. §§ 15-10-40 et seq. Since most dispossessory actions are prosecuted in Magistrate Court, for convenience, these Code Sections are reproduced in Appendix B.

[42] See Appendix D.

[43] O.C.G.A. § 44-7-54.

At the conclusion of the trial, the landlord's foremost goal in a dispossessory action is the entry and issuance of a writ of possession. If the tenant has filed an answer within the time allowed by law and appears for trial, the writ will issue seven (7) days after the landlord prevails at trial.[44] If the tenant fails to file an answer and allows a default judgment to be taken against him, the writ will issue immediately.[45] If the tenant files an answer but fails to appear for trial, the landlord should move to strike the answer and for a default judgment (which motion the trial court will generally grant), in which case the writ will issue immediately. Note that once the writ is issued, it still must be "executed," which is the actual eviction process itself.[46]

If the landlord has obtained personal service on the tenant, has sought a money judgment against the tenant, and has proven the amount of his damages to the trial court's satisfaction, then the trial court is authorized to issue a money judgment against the tenant, in addition to the writ of possession. Collection of the judgment is the landlord's responsibility, and the various means by which one might collect a judgment is well beyond the scope of this book. However, one administrative step the landlord can take is to ask the trial court to include a direction that the clerk of court will immediately issue a writ of *fieri facias* upon the judgment, to enable the landlord to record the judgment of record wherever the tenant might own property, both now and in the future.[47] In addition, if the tenant ever pays his rent by check, the prudent landlord will keep a photocopy of the check in the tenant's file, so that the landlord will know of one place to potentially look for funds in a future garnishment proceeding.

Practice Pointer #16: The landlord who successfully obtains a money judgment against the tenant should ask the Court to order that a writ of fieri facias should be issued immediately.

Practice Pointer #17: The landlord should have kept a copy of at least one check from the tenant, to give him a possible avenue of garnishment.

The landlord might view the security deposit paid at the beginning of the lease period as an obvious avenue of collection of a money judgment against the tenant, but the landlord must be extremely careful in how he handles the security deposit, lest he expose himself to liability to the tenant for wrongfully withholding the security deposit. At the beginning of the lease period, the landlord should have provided the tenant with a list of all non-latent defects in the premises, which the tenant approves by signing the same. The security deposit is ostensibly required to be returned to the tenant within one month after the landlord recovers possession of the premises, except that the landlord is allowed to retain that portion of the security deposit which covers repairs beyond the existing damages, and beyond "normal wear and tear." In addition, the landlord may retain a portion of the security deposit to cover non-payment of rent or utility charges, and actual damages caused by the tenant's breach (if the landlord acts to mitigate those damages) – but only if the lease agreement so provides. The landlord should therefore be sure to draft a provision into the lease agreement specifically addressing and describing the circumstances under which the security deposit will be retained.

> **Practice Pointer #18: The landlord should not apply any portion of the security deposit paid by the tenant to past-due rent unless the lease agreement specifically allows him to do so.**

---

[44] O.C.G.A. § 44-7-55(a).

[45] O.C.G.A. § 44-7-53(a).

[46] See Chapter 8.

[47] See Appendix D.

Achieving victory at trial is usually, but not always, the end of the litigation. In some cases, one party might file an appeal, seeking either a retrial or a reversal of whatever decision the trial court made. A full explanation of the nuances of appellate practice in Georgia is beyond the scope of this book. There are, however, a number of basic concepts with which the landlord should be familiar regarding the appeal of a dispossessory action.

Default Judgments. There is no appeal from a default judgment. A default judgment occurs whenever the tenant fails to file an answer. A default judgment is also entered if the tenant files an answer which is then struck for some reason, most likely because he fails to appear for trial.

Judgments Reached After Trial. If the judgment is not a default judgment, the case may be appealed by the losing party – landlord or tenant – as with any other case. If the trial court is a Magistrate Court, the losing party has the right to an appeal and a trial de novo in the State or Superior Court of the same county.[48] If the trial court is a court of record, that is, a State or Superior Court, then the losing party may appeal to the Georgia Court of Appeals, either directly or by application, as is appropriate for the particular case. An appeal from a State or Superior Court which itself was acting as an appellate court in the case will always require an application to the Court of Appeals.

Appeal by Tenant. In the event of an appeal by the tenant, the landlord may ask the court to require the tenant to pay rent into the court registry pending the outcome of the appeal, which will be paid to the landlord if and when he prevails on the appeal. The trial court may include this requirement in its original judgment as a contingent requirement of the tenant who elects to file an appeal, and the prudent landlord will ask the trial court to include such a requirement at the conclusion of the trial.

> **Practice Pointer #19: The landlord should always ask the trial court to include a provision in the judgment requiring the tenant to continue to pay rent into the court registry as a condition of maintaining an appeal.**

Preserving the Record in Magistrate Court. If the trial court is a Magistrate Court, the evidence introduced at trial will likely be returned to the parties, rather than made a part of the court's file. In the event the landlord introduced evidence which was not attached to his affidavit or otherwise previously made a part of the court's file, in practice the landlord can sometimes still make such evidence a part of the court's file by filing a supplemental affidavit (with the documents attached) with the clerk of court after the trial. Although the trial court or the appellate court is free to ignore the supplemental affidavit and the attachments thereto, this practice is recommended as a way of helping perfect what is otherwise an unperfectable record.

Practice Pointer #20: The landlord should try to ensure all evidence introduced at trial in the Magistrate Court is somehow filed into that court's file, by filing a post-trial affidavit with exhibits attached, if necessary.

---

[48] Recall from Chapter 2 that a trial de novo means the second court will start all over again when it hears the case, rather than starting from the record from which the appeal was taken, effectively giving the appealing party a retrial of his case.

Once a landlord has tried his case, won, and been issued a writ of possession, and no appeal is filed (or the appeal is resolved favorably to the landlord), the writ must be "executed" by the sheriff or marshal in the county where the writ was issued. Some effort will be required to coordinate the execution of the writ with the actual removal of the person and property from the rented premises, as the sheriff or marshal will not provide the labor necessary to remove the property. The prudent landlord will also hire a locksmith to attend the eviction, to change the locks on the rented premises at the same time the tenant and his property are removed.

The landlord is not entitled to retain the tenant's personal property upon the eviction. The landlord is also not responsible for said property, however. After the writ is executed, it is sufficient for the tenant's property to be removed from the rented premises and stacked on the street or sidewalk, so long as passage is not obstructed. Note the landlord bears the costs associated with the actual eviction.

In practice, especially in larger counties, the sheriff or marshal has such a significant backlog of writs of execution (to say nothing of other matters) that it could be several weeks after the writ issues before he is able to execute the same. If this is the case, retaining an eviction servicing company can be extremely beneficial. In addition to providing the labor and logistical support for actually carrying out the eviction, it is not uncommon for an eviction servicing company to have an "in" with the local authorities, which can help expedite the execution on the writ. Whether the use of an eviction servicing company makes good economic sense in a particular case will depend on the timing and circumstances of that case and is therefore left as an exercise for the reader.

Practice Pointer #21: The landlord should investigate how long it will take to have the writ of possession executed by the county sheriff or marshal, and he should consider hiring an eviction servicing company if appropriate.

Not all cases go to trial, and in fact a growing number of cases are resolved short of trial via "alternative dispute resolution" ("ADR"). The ever-increasing burden on the courts has resulted in many courts developing programs for submission of cases to ADR, usually as a pretrial requirement. There are several different forms of ADR, including mediation, arbitration, early case evaluation, and so on. The purpose of this chapter is not to exhaustively explain the nuances of ADR. Rather, this chapter is provided to give a basic overview of ADR as it relates to dispossessory cases.

Arbitration. In a complex, high-stakes, commercial lease context, and if the lease agreement so provides, arbitration may be a viable option. Arbitration looks, at first blush, much like a bench trial. There are parties, witnesses, and evidence, and there is a referee (the arbitrator) who will ultimately make a decision. The process is usually much more streamlined than a full-blown trial, however, and there are virtually none of the formalities such as civil practice or evidentiary rules. There is one catch, though – it is almost impossible to appeal from an adverse result in an arbitration.

Mediation. In the overwhelming majority of cases, the primary form of ADR which will be available is mediation. Mediation is essentially an assisted settlement conference. There are no rules of evidence, and the proceedings themselves are generally confidential. In addition, during the mediation process, parties will have an opportunity to consult privately with the mediator, whose function is to explore the strengths and weaknesses of each side's case and assist the parties in reaching a compromise of their disputed issues. Although mediation is not binding (unlike arbitration), courts are increasingly requiring parties to attempt mediation before proceeding to trial, especially in landlord-tenant cases. In addition, if a settlement is reached, the courts typically will enforce the terms of the settlement, which can include rights and obligations to which the parties may agree to submit, but which the court could not impose otherwise by order or judgment.

In the landlord-tenant context, several of the larger counties in Georgia have developed their own court-connected mediation programs, through which mediators are made available by the court, and to which either the parties can elect or the court may require the case to be submitted. Fulton County, for example, has the highest-volume landlord-tenant court in the state, with trial calendars routinely running two days per week. That court typically calls two calendars on each trial date – an earlier "mediation" calendar, which is comprised of all contested cases in which a tenant has filed an answer which asserts at least one defense, and a later "trial" calendar, which is comprised of all other types of pending cases. If a case is called in the "mediation" calendar, but does not result in a settlement, that case will be reset for the "trial" calendar that same day. Similarly, in other counties (e.g., Gwinnett County), mediators may be available on a first-come-first-served basis, and if the parties request a mediator during the calendar call, then the case will be referred to mediation, and tried that day if the case is not resolved in mediation.

A typical mediation opens with a "joint session," attended by the mediator and all of the parties (and their attorneys, if they have attorneys). The mediator will explain the ground rules for mediation, and in most cases all participants sign an agreement to mediate. The joint session then typically proceeds with uninterrupted opening statements by each of the parties in turn, starting with the plaintiff (i.e., the landlord). The joint session may be followed by "caucuses" between the mediator and one of the parties, outside the presence of the other party. Caucuses are confidential, and the mediator is typically bound not to reveal anything said in caucus to the other party, unless expressly authorized to do so. How the mediation proceeds is generally up to the mediator, who will typically go back and forth between the parties until a resolution is reached or an impasse is declared. If a settlement is reached, it is reduced to writing and signed by all of the parties. If the form of the settlement is a consent judgment or a consent order,[49] it will be signed by the trial judge and entered as any other order.

Determining Whether a Case Is Appropriate for Mediation. Every contested landlord-tenant case should be submitted to mediation, if possible. Even in a case that does not settle (or maybe could never have been expected to settle), mediation is generally valuable for at least four reasons. First, the joint session gives each party a chance to state his case. An observant litigant will pay close attention to the opposing party's statement of his case, as this can provide insight into the case that party will present at trial if the case does not settle. Second, mediation will typically result in a narrowing of the issues for trial, which will make the trial itself more efficient. Third, any documents and other evidence can and should be exchanged during mediation, which will also make the trial proceed more quickly and efficiently. Finally, trial courts are more likely to award attorney's fees if the party who prevails at trial can demonstrate that the result at trial is not appreciably better than (or may even be worse than) the compromise offered by that party during settlement negotiations – in other words, the trial court is more likely to award litigation expenses if it thinks the losing party wasted the court's time.

> **Practice Pointer #22: The prudent landlord will attempt mediation if possible and will keep an open mind throughout the mediation process, even if it seems obvious the case will not settle.**

In addition to the foregoing, there is one other consideration that the trial lawyer, in particular, should keep in mind. In a typical landlord-tenant case, especially a residential lease case, although the landlord may be represented by counsel, the tenant is usually *pro se* and is often more interested in having his "day in court" than in actually achieving any substantive relief. Thus, while an experienced attorney may perceive – quite correctly – that there is no legal merit to the tenant's position, the tenant may feel better and become more cooperative once he has had a chance to "make his case," and the opportunity to present his case to the mediator may be sufficient in the tenant's mind. The trial lawyer would do well to keep this in mind, if for no other reason than the very pragmatic reality that the mediation may produce the same result as the trial, without having to waste half a day or more watching a trial judge dispose of other cases before his case is ultimately reached for trial.

> **Practice Pointer #23: Counsel for the landlord should consider using mediation to give a pro se tenant his proverbial "day in court."**

Achieving Efficiency in Mediation. In most courts which provide mediators and/or require cases to be submitted to mediation, the mediator's time will be quite limited. (For an anecdotal example from the author's own experience as a mediator in Fulton County's program, a typical mediation calendar might include eighty cases, which are intended to be processed by ten mediators in a two-hour window, meaning an average of fifteen minutes could be devoted to each case.) The parties, therefore, should be focused on maximizing the use of that time, to achieve the greatest value in the mediation.

To achieve this end, the parties should keep in mind the most important objective for each party. For the landlord, the most important objective is typically possession; although payment of past-due rent and other charges can be significant, most landlords will be focused on "stopping the bleeding" by recovering possession as quickly as possible. A tenant, on the other hand, typically has two major concerns – retaining possession of the premises as long as possible, and minimizing his financial exposure. Proper trial preparation should make it fairly obvious in most cases which party is going to prevail at trial and will thus have the most leverage in the mediation.

From the landlord's perspective, it may well be that the landlord is only really interested in possession so that he can find another tenant who will be more diligent in paying his rent. If the tenant is willing and able to pay over time, but cannot pay as required by the lease, it may be beneficial to explore an alternate payment schedule. In such a case, a consent order which sets forth such a schedule, and simultaneously grants the landlord the ability to obtain a writ of possession immediately upon his affidavit certifying a missed payment (i.e., without the need to come back to court for a trial), may be a sufficient compromise.[50]

Another common scenario is a situation in which the tenant is capable of paying but is unwilling to do so because of a failure (real or perceived) of the landlord to perform some specified repair, whereas the landlord is willing to make the repair but is unwilling to do so because he does not trust the tenant to pay his rent – an understandable concern, but not a legal excuse for failing to maintain the premises. In such a case, it might be possible for the parties to agree (via consent order) that the tenant will deposit the rent into the registry of the court, the landlord will perform the specified repairs, and then the landlord will be entitled to draw down the funds in the registry upon the tenant's satisfaction that the repairs have been completed. A Magistrate Court will typically have the authority and ability to enforce a consent order of this type, even though it may include forms of relief which it would not be authorized to independently order or award if the case proceeded to trial.

---

[49] See Appendix D.

[50] See Appendix D.

Postscript

With proper preparation and attention to detail, and perhaps a little luck along the way, most landlords should find the dispossessory process to be relatively simple and straightforward, and the landlord should generally be able to achieve good results from following the process correctly.

Several appendices are included for the reader's convenience, including copies of the statutory text governing dispossessory law and procedure, as well as civil procedure applicable in the Magistrate Court. Also included are numerous examples of forms that may be useful to the landlord, from standard correspondence and pleadings to settlement agreements and consent orders. [These forms are available as plain text files, for free, at this book's web site, www.GeorgiaEvictionBook.com.] There is also a convenient summary of all of the Practice Pointers which have appeared throughout the text. Finally, a condensed checklist summarizing the entire dispossessory process has also been included (and, once again, is freely available from the book's web site).

Good luck!

Appendix A

Official Code of Georgia Annotated
Title 44 – Property
Chapter 7 – Landlord and Tenant

The following are excerpts from the Georgia Code describing landlord-tenant law in Georgia.

Article 1. In General

§ 44-7-1. *Relation of landlord and tenant exists, when; leases for less than five years*

§ 44-7-2. *How relationship created*

§ 44-7-5. *Implied contract to pay rent*

§ 44-7-6. *Tenancy at will when no time specified*

§ 44-7-7. *Notice to terminate tenancy at will*

§ 44-7-9. *Estoppel to dispute landlord's title or to attorn to another*

§ 44-7-10. *Delivery of possession*

§ 44-7-11. *Rights of tenants*

§ 44-7-12. *Removal of trade fixtures by tenant*

§ 44-7-13. *Repairs and improvements, duties as to*

§ 44-7-14. *Liability of landlord for negligence of tenant and for failure to repair*

§ 44-7-14.1. *Unlawful to suspend furnishing of utilities to tenant until final disposition of dispossessory proceeding*

§ 44-7-15. *Casualties not to abate rent*

Article 1. In General

§ 44-7-1. *Relation of landlord and tenant exists, when; leases for less than five years*

    (a) The relationship of landlord and tenant is created when the owner of real estate grants to another person, who accepts such grant, the right simply to possess and enjoy the use of such real estate either for a fixed time or at the will of the grantor. In such a case, no estate passes out of the landlord and the tenant has only a usufruct which may not be conveyed except by the landlord's consent and which is not subject to levy and sale.

    (b) All renting or leasing of real estate for a period of time less than five years shall be held to convey only the right to possess and enjoy such real estate, to pass no estate out of the landlord, and to give only the usufruct unless the contrary is agreed upon by the parties to the contract and is so stated in the contract.

§ 44-7-2. *How relationship created*

    (a) Contracts creating the relationship of landlord and tenant for any time not exceeding one year may be by parol.

    (b) In any contract, lease, license agreement, or similar

agreement, oral or written, for the use or rental of real property as a dwelling place, a landlord or a tenant may not waive, assign, transfer, or otherwise avoid any of the rights, duties, or remedies contained in the following provisions of law:

(1) Code Section 44-7-13, relating to the duties of a landlord as to repairs and improvements;

(2) Code Section 44-7-14, relating to the liability of a landlord for failure to repair;

(3) Ordinances adopted pursuant to Code Section 36-61-11;

(4) Article 3 of this chapter, relating to proceedings against tenants holding over;

(5) Article 4 of this chapter, relating to distress warrants;

(6) Article 2 of this chapter, relating to security deposits; and

(7) Any applicable provision of Chapter 11 of Title 9 which has not been superseded by this chapter.

(c) A provision for the payment by the tenant of the attorney's fees of the landlord upon the breach of a rental agreement by the tenant, which provision is contained in a contract, lease, license agreement, or similar agreement, oral or written, for the use or rental of real property as a dwelling place shall be void unless the provision also provides for the payment by the landlord of the attorney's fees of the tenant upon the breach of the rental agreement by the landlord.

§ 44-7-5. Implied contract to pay rent

When, in an action for rent, title is shown in the plaintiff and occupation by the defendant is proved, an obligation to pay rent is generally implied. However, if the entry of the defendant on the premises was not under the plaintiff or if the possession of the defendant is adverse to the plaintiff, no such implication arises.

§ 44-7-6. Tenancy at will when no time specified

Where no time is specified for the termination of a tenancy, the law construes it to be a tenancy at will.

§ 44-7-7. *Notice to terminate tenancy at will*

Sixty days' notice from the landlord or 30 days' notice from the tenant is necessary to terminate a tenancy at will.

§ 44-7-9. *Estoppel to dispute landlord's title or to attorn to another*

The tenant may not dispute his landlord's title or attorn to another claimant while he is in actual physical occupation, while he is performing any active or passive act or taking any position whereby he expressly or impliedly recognizes his landlord's title, or while he is taking any position that is inconsistent with the position that the landlord's title is defective.

§ 44-7-10. *Delivery of possession*

The tenant shall deliver possession to the landlord at the expiration of his term; and, if he fails or refuses to do so, a summary remedy pursuant to Article 3 of this chapter is given to the landlord.

§ 44-7-11. *Rights of tenants*

The tenant has no rights beyond the use of the land and tenements rented to him and such privileges as are necessary for the enjoyment of his use. He may not cut or destroy growing trees, remove permanent fixtures, or otherwise injure the property. He may use dead or fallen timber for firewood and the pasturage for his cattle.

§ 44-7-12. *Removal of trade fixtures by tenant*

During the term of his tenancy or any continuation thereof or while he is in possession under the landlord, a tenant may remove trade fixtures erected by him. After the term and his possession are ended, any trade fixtures remaining will be regarded as abandoned for the use of the landlord and will become the landlord's property.

§ 44-7-13. *Repairs and improvements, duties as to*

The landlord must keep the premises in repair. He shall be liable for all substantial improvements placed upon the premises by his consent.

§ 44-7-14. Liability of landlord for negligence of tenant and for failure to repair

Having fully parted with possession and the right of possession, the landlord is not responsible to third persons for damages resulting from the negligence or illegal use of the premises by the tenant; provided, however, the landlord is responsible for damages arising from defective construction or for damages arising from the failure to keep the premises in repair.

§ 44-7-14.1. Unlawful to suspend furnishing of utilities to tenant until final disposition of dispossessory proceeding

(a) As used in this Code section, the term "utilities" means heat, light, and water service.

(b) It shall be unlawful for any landlord knowingly and willfully to suspend the furnishing of utilities to a tenant until after the final disposition of any dispossessory proceeding by the landlord against such tenant.

(c) Any person who violates subsection (b) of this Code section shall, upon conviction, be assessed a fine not to exceed $500.00.

§ 44-7-15. Casualties not to abate rent

The destruction of a tenement by fire or the loss of possession by any casualty not caused by the landlord or from a defect of his title shall not abate the rent contracted to be paid.

§ 44-7-16. Interest on rent contracts

All contracts for rent shall bear interest from the time the rent is due.

§ 44-7-22. Termination of residential rental or lease agreements; active duty service members

(a) As used in this Code section, the term "service member" means an active duty member of the regular or reserve component of the United States armed forces, the United States Coast Guard, the Georgia National Guard, or the Georgia Air National Guard on ordered federal duty for a period of 90 days or longer.

(b) Any service member may terminate his or her residential rental or lease agreement by providing the landlord with a written notice of termination to be effective on the date stated in the notice that is at least 30 days after the landlord's receipt of the notice if any of the following criteria are met:

(1) The service member is required, pursuant to a permanent change of station orders, to move 35 miles or more from the location of the rental premises;

(2) The service member is released from active duty or state active duty after having leased the rental premises while on active duty status and the rental premises is 35 miles or more from the service member's home of record prior to entering active duty;

(3) After entering into a rental agreement, the service member receives military orders requiring him or her to move into government quarters;

(4) After entering into a rental agreement, the service member becomes eligible to live in government quarters and the failure to move into government quarters will result in a forfeiture of the service member's basic allowance for housing;

(5) The service member receives temporary duty orders, temporary change of station orders, or state active duty orders to an area 35 miles or more from the location of the rental premises, provided such orders are for a period exceeding 60 days; or

(6) The service member has leased the property but prior to taking possession of the rental premises receives a change of orders to an area that is 35 miles or more from the location of the rental premises.

(c) The notice to the landlord pursuant to subsection (b) of this Code section shall be accompanied by either a copy of the official military orders or a written verification signed by the service member's commanding officer.

(d) In the event a service member dies during active duty, an adult member of his or her immediate family may terminate the service member's residential rental or lease agreement by providing the landlord with a written notice of termination to be effective on the date stated in the notice that is at least 30 days after the landlord's receipt of the notice. The notice to the landlord must be accompanied by either a copy of the official military orders showing the service member was on active duty or a written verification signed by the service member's commanding officer and a copy of the service member's death certificate.

(e) Upon termination of a rental agreement under this Code section, the service member is liable for the rent due under the rental agreement prorated to the effective date of the termination payable at such time as would have otherwise been required by the terms of the rental agreement. The service member is not liable for any other rent or damages due to the early termination of the tenancy as provided for in this Code section. Notwithstanding any provision of law to the contrary, if a service member terminates the rental agreement pursuant to this Code section 14 or more days prior to occupancy, no damages or penalties of any kind will be assessable.

(f) The provisions of this Code section shall apply to all residential rental or lease agreements entered into on or after July 1, 2005, and to any renewals, modifications, or extensions of such agreements in effect on such date. The provisions of this Code section may not be waived or modified by the agreement of the parties under any circumstances.

Article 2. Security Deposits
§ 44-7-30. *Definitions*

As used in this article, the term:

(1) "Nonrefundable fee" means any money or other consideration paid or given by a tenant to a landlord under the terms of a residential rental agreement which the parties agreed would not be refunded.

(2) "Residential rental agreement" means a contract, lease,

or license agreement for the rental or use of real property as a dwelling place.

(3) "Security deposit" means money or any other form of security given after July 1, 1976, by a tenant to a landlord which shall be held by the landlord on behalf of a tenant by virtue of a residential rental agreement and shall include, but not be limited to, damage deposits, advance rent deposits, and pet deposits. Such term shall not include nonrefundable fees, or money or other consideration which are not to be returned to the tenant under the terms of the residential rental agreement or which were to be applied toward the payment of rent or reimbursement of services or utilities provided to the tenant.

§ 44-7-31. Security deposits to be placed in escrow accounts

Except as provided in Code Section 44-7-32, whenever a security deposit is held by a landlord or such landlord's agent on behalf of a tenant, such security deposit shall be deposited in an escrow account established only for that purpose in any bank or lending institution subject to regulation by this state or any agency of the United States government. The security deposit shall be held in trust for the tenant by the landlord or such landlord's agent except as provided in Code Section 44-7-34. Tenants shall be informed in writing of the location of the escrow account required by this Code section.

§ 44-7-32. Surety bond in lieu of escrow account

(a) As an alternative to the requirement that security deposits be placed in escrow as provided in Code Section 44-7-31, the landlord may post and maintain an effective surety bond with the clerk of the superior court in the county in which the dwelling unit is located. The amount of the bond shall be the total amount of the security deposits which the landlord holds on behalf of the tenants or $50,000.00, whichever is less. The bond shall be executed by the landlord as principal and a surety company authorized and licensed to do business in this state as surety. The bond shall be conditioned upon the faithful compliance of the landlord with Code Section 44-7-34 and the return of the security deposits in the event of the bankruptcy of the landlord or foreclosure of the premises and shall run to the benefit of any tenant injured by the landlord's violation of Code Section 44-7-34.

(b) The surety may withdraw from the bond by giving 30 days' written notice by registered or certified mail or statutory overnight delivery to the clerk of the superior court in the county in which the principal's dwelling unit is located, provided that such withdrawal shall not release the surety from any liability existing under the bond at the time of the effective date of the withdrawal.

(c) The clerk of the superior court shall receive a fee of $5.00 for filing and recording the surety bond and shall also receive a fee of $5.00 for canceling the surety bond. The clerk of the superior court shall not be held personally liable should the surety bond prove to be invalid.

§ 44-7-33. *List of existing damages; inspection of premises at termination; list of damages, dissent from; action to recover security deposit*

(a) Prior to tendering a security deposit, the tenant shall be presented with a comprehensive list of any existing damage to the premises, which list shall be for the tenant's permanent retention. The tenant shall have the right to inspect the premises to ascertain the accuracy of the list prior to taking occupancy. The landlord and the tenant shall sign the list and this shall be conclusive evidence of the accuracy of the list but shall not be conclusive as to latent defects. If the tenant refuses to sign the list, the tenant shall state specifically in writing the items on the list to which he dissents and shall sign such statement of dissent.

(b) Within three business days after the date of the termination of occupancy, the landlord or his agent shall inspect the premises and compile a comprehensive list of any damage done to the premises which is the basis for any charge against the security deposit and the estimated dollar value of such damage. The tenant shall have the right to inspect the premises within five business days after the termination of the occupancy in order to ascertain the accuracy of the list. The landlord and the tenant shall sign the list, and this shall be conclusive evidence of the accuracy of the list. If the tenant refuses to sign the list, he shall state specifically in writing the items on the list to which he dissents and shall sign such statement of dissent. If the tenant terminates occupancy without notifying the landlord, the landlord may make a final inspection within a reasonable time after discovering the termination of occupancy.

(c) A tenant who disputes the accuracy of the final damage list given pursuant to subsection (b) of this Code section may bring an action in any courtofcompetentjurisdiction in this state to recover the portion of the security deposit which the tenant believes to be wrongfully withheld for damages to the premises. The tenant's claims shall be limited to those items to which the tenant specifically dissented in accordance with this Code section. If the tenant fails to sign a list or to dissent specifically in accordance with this Code section, the tenant shall not be entitled to recover the security deposit or any other damages under Code Section 44-7-35, provided that the lists required under this Code section contain written notice of the tenant's duty to sign or to dissent to the list.

§ 44-7-34. *Return of security deposit*

(a) Except as otherwise provided in this article, within one month after the termination of the residential lease or the surrender and acceptance of the premises, whichever occurs last, a landlord shall return to the tenant the full security deposit which was deposited with the landlord by the tenant. No security deposit shall be retained to cover ordinary wear and tear which occurred as a result of the use of the premises for the purposes for which the premises were intended, provided that there was no negligence, carelessness, accident, or abuse of the premises by the tenant or members of his household or their invitees or guests. In the event that actual cause exists for retaining any portion of the security deposit, the landlord shall provide the tenant with a written statement listing the exact reasons for the retention thereof. If the reason for retention is based on damages to the premises, such damages shall be listed as provided in Code Section 44-7-33. When the statement is delivered, it shall be accompanied by a payment of the difference between any sum deposited and the amount retained. The landlord shall be deemed to have complied with this Code section by mailing the statement and any payment required to the last known address of the tenant via first class mail. If the letter containing the payment is returned to the landlord undelivered and if the landlord is unable to locate the tenant after reasonable effort, the payment shall become the property of the landlord 90 days after the date the payment was mailed. Nothing in this Code section shall preclude the landlord from retaining the security deposit for nonpayment of rent or of fees for late payment, for abandonment of the premises, for nonpayment of utility charges, for repair work or cleaning contracted for by the tenant with third parties, for unpaid pet fees, or for actual damages caused by the tenant's breach, provided the landlord attempts to mitigate the actual damages.

(b) In any court action in which there is a determination that neither the landlord nor the tenant is entitled to all or a portion of a security deposit under this article, the judge or the jury, as the case may be, shall determine what would be an equitable disposition of the security deposit; and the judge shall order the security deposit paid in accordance with such disposition.

§ 44-7-35. *Remedies for noncompliance of landlord*

(a) A landlord shall not be entitled to retain any portion of a security deposit if the security deposit was not deposited in an escrow account in accordance with Code

Section 44-7-31 or a surety bond was not posted in accordance with Code Section 44-7-32 and if the initial and final damage lists required by Code Section 44-7-33 are not made and provided to the tenant.

(b) The failure of a landlord to provide each of the written statements within the time periods specified in Code Sections 44-7-33 and 44-7-34 shall work a forfeiture of all his rights to withhold any portion of the security deposit or to bring an action against the tenant for damages to the premises.

(c) Any landlord who fails to return any part of a security deposit which is required to be returned to a tenant pursuant to this article shall be liable to the tenant in the amount of three times the sum improperly withheld plus reasonable attorney's fees; provided, however, that the landlord shall be liable only for the sum erroneously withheld if the landlord shows by the preponderance of the evidence that the withholding was not intentional and resulted from a bona fide error which occurred in spite of the existence of procedures reasonably designed to avoid such errors.

§ 44-7-36. *Exemptions*

Code Sections 44-7-31, 44-7-32, 44-7-33, and 44-7-35 shall not apply to rental units which are owned by a natural person if such natural person, his or her spouse, and his or her minor children collectively own ten or fewer rental units; provided, however, that this exemption does not apply to units for which management, including rent collection, is performed by third persons, natural or otherwise, for a fee.

§ 44-7-37. *Limitation on rent liability of military personnel*

Notwithstanding any other provision of this chapter, if a person is on active duty with the United States military and enters into a residential lease of property for occupancy by that person or that person's immediate family and subsequently receives permanent change of station orders or temporary duty orders for a period in excess of three months, any liability of the person for rent under the lease may not exceed:

(1) Thirty days' rent after written notice and proof of the assignment are given to the landlord; and

(2) The cost of repairing damage to the premises caused by an act or omission of the tenant.

Article 3. Dispossessory Proceedings
§ 44-7-49. Writ of possession; limitations

As used in this article, the term "writ of possession" means a writ issued to recover the possession of land or other property and such writ shall not contain restrictions, responsibilities, or conditions upon the landlord in order to be placed in full possession of the land or other property.

§ 44-7-50. Demand for possession; proceedings on tenant's refusal to deliver

(a) In all cases where a tenant holds possession of lands or tenements over and beyond the term for which they were rented or leased to the tenant or fails to pay the rent when it becomes due and in all cases where lands or tenements are held and occupied by any tenant at will or sufferance, whether under contract of rent or not, when the owner of the lands or tenements desires possession of the lands or tenements, the owner may, individually or by an agent, attorney in fact, or attorney at law, demand the possession of the property so rented, leased, held, or occupied. If the tenant refuses or fails to deliver possession when so demanded, the owner or the agent, attorney at law, or attorney in fact of the owner may immediately go before the judge of the superior court, the judge of the state court, or the clerk or deputy clerk of either court, or the judge or the clerk or deputy clerk of any other court with jurisdiction over the subject matter, or a magistrate in the district where the land lies and make an affidavit under oath to the facts. The affidavit may likewise be made before a notary public, subject to the same requirements for judicial approval specified in Code Section 18-4-61, relating to garnishment affidavits.

(b) If issued by a public housing authority, the demand for possession required by subsection (a) of this Code section may be provided concurrently with the federally required notice of lease termination in a separate writing.

§ 44-7-51. *Summons to be served on defendant; time to answer; defenses and counterclaims*

(a) When the affidavit provided for in Code Section 44-7- 50 is made, the judge of the superior court, the state court, or any other court with jurisdiction over the subject matter or the judge, clerk, or deputy clerk of the magistrate court shall grant and issue a summons to the sheriff or his deputy or to any lawful constable of the county where the land is located. A copy of the summons and a copy of the affidavit shall be personally served upon the defendant. If the sheriff is unable to serve the defendant personally, service may be had by delivering the summons and the affidavit to any person who is sui juris residing on the premises or, if after reasonable effort no such person is found residing on the premises, by posting a copy of the summons and the affidavit on the door of the premises and, on the same day of such posting, by enclosing, directing, stamping, and mailing by first-class mail a copy of the summons and the affidavit to the defendant at his last known address, if any, and making an entry of this action on the affidavit filed in the case.

(b) The summons served on the defendant pursuant to subsection (a) of this Code section shall command and require the tenant to answer either orally or in writing within seven days from the date of the actual service unless the seventh day is a Saturday, a Sunday, or a legal holiday, in which case the answer may be made on the next day which is not a Saturday, a Sunday, or a legal holiday. If the answer is oral, the substance thereof shall be endorsed on the dispossessory affidavit. The answer may contain any legal or equitable defense or counterclaim. The landlord need not appear on the date of the tenant's response. The last possible date to answer shall be stated on the summons.

(c) If service is by posting a copy of the summons and the affidavit on the door of the premises and mailing a copy of the summons and the affidavit to the defendant, as provided in subsection (a) of this Code section, the court shall have jurisdiction to enter a default judgment for possession of the premises in the absence of an answer being filed, but in such instance a default judgment for money owed may not be entered unless the defendant files an answer or otherwise makes an appearance in the case.

§ 44-7-52. *Offer of payment by the tenant*

(a) Except as provided in subsection (c) of this Code section, in an action for nonpayment of rent, the tenant shall be allowed to tender to the landlord, within seven days of the day the tenant was served with the summons pursuant to Code Section 44-7-51, all rents allegedly owed plus the cost of the dispossessory warrant. Such a tender shall be a complete defense to the action; provided, however, that a landlord is required to accept such a tender from any individual tenant after the issuance of a dispossessory summons only once in any 12 month period.

(b) If the court finds that the tenant is entitled to prevail on the defense provided in subsection (a) of this Code section and the landlord refused the tender as provided under subsection (a) of this Code section, the court shall issue an order requiring the tenant to pay to the landlord all rents which are owed by the tenant and the costs of the dispossessory warrant within three days of said order. Upon failure of the tenant to pay such sum, a writ of possession shall issue. Such payment shall not count as a tender pursuant to subsection (a) of this Code section.

(c) For a tenant who is not a tenant under a residential rental agreement as defined in Code Section 44-7-30, tender and acceptance of less than all rents allegedly owed plus the cost of the dispossessory warrant shall not be a bar nor a defense to an action brought under Code Section 44-7-50 but shall, upon proof of same, be considered by the trial court when awarding damages.

§ 44-7-53. *Failure to answer; issuance of writ of possession; answer and trial*

(a) If the tenant fails to answer as provided in subsection (b) of Code Section 44-7-51, the court shall issue a writ of possession instanter notwithstanding Code Section 9-11-55 or Code Section 9-11-62. The court, without the intervention of a jury, shall not require any further evidence nor hold any hearings and the plaintiff shall be entitled to a verdict and judgment by default for all rents due as if every item and paragraph of the affidavit provided for in Code Section 44-7-50 were supported by proper evidence.

(b) If the tenant answers, a trial of the issues shall be had in accordance with the procedure prescribed for civil actions in courts of record except that if the action is tried in the magistrate court the trial shall be had in accordance with the procedures prescribed for that court. Every effort should be made by the trial court to expedite a trial of the issues. The defendant shall be allowed to remain in possession of the premises pending the final outcome of the litigation; provided, however, that, at the time of his answer, the tenant must pay rent into the registry of the court pursuant to Code Section 44-7-54.

§ 44-7-54. *Payment of rent into court*

(a) In any case where the issue of the right of possession cannot be finally determined within two weeks from the date of service of the copy of the summons and the copy of the affidavit, the tenant shall be required to pay into the registry of the trial court:

(1) All rent and utility payments which are the responsibility of the tenant payable to the landlord under terms of the lease which become due after the issu-

ance of the dispossessory warrant, said rent and utility payments to be paid as such become due. If the landlord and the tenant disagree as to the amount of rent, either or both of them may submit to the court any written rental contract for the purpose of establishing the amount of rent to be paid into the registry of the court. If the amount of rent is in controversy and no written rental agreement exists between the tenant and landlord, the court shall require the amount of rent to be a sum equal to the last previous rental payment made by the tenant and accepted by the landlord without written objection; and

(2) All rent and utility payments which are the responsibility of the tenant payable to the landlord under terms of the lease allegedly owed prior to the issuance of the dispossessory warrant; provided, however, that, in lieu of such payment, the tenant shall be allowed to submit to the court a receipt indicating that payment has been made to the landlord. In the event that the amount of rent is in controversy, the court shall determine the amount of rent to be paid into court in the same manner as provided in paragraph (1) of this subsection.

(b) If the tenant should fail to make any payment as it becomes due pursuant to paragraph (1) or (2) of subsection (a) of this Code section, the court shall issue a writ of possession and the landlord shall be placed in full possession of the premises by the sheriff, the deputy, or the constable.

(c) The court shall order the clerk of the court to pay to the landlord the payments claimed under the rental contracts paid into the registry of the court as said payments are made; provided, however, that, if the tenant claims that he or she is entitled to all or any part of the funds and such claim is an issue of controversy in the litigation, the court shall order the clerk to pay to the landlord without delay only that portion of the funds to which the tenant has made no claim in the proceedings or may make such other order as is appropriate under the circumstances. That part of the funds which is a matter of controversy in the litigation shall remain in the registry of the court until a determination of the issues by the trial court. If either party appeals the decision of the trial court, that part of the funds equal to any sums found by the trial court to be due from the landlord to the tenant shall remain in the registry of the court until a final determination of the issues. The court shall order the clerk to pay to the landlord without delay the remaining funds in court and all payments of future rent made into court pursuant to paragraph (1) of subsection (a) of this Code section unless the tenant can show good cause that some or all of such payments should remain in court pending a final determination of the issues.

§ 44-7-55. *Judgment and satisfaction*

(a) If, on the trial of the case, the judgment is against the tenant, judgment shall be entered against the tenant for all rents due and for any other claim relating to the dispute. The court shall issue a writ of possession, both of execution for the judgment amount and a writ to be effective at the expiration of seven days after the date such judgment was entered, except as otherwise provided in Code Section 44-7-56.

(b) If the judgment is for the tenant, he shall be entitled to remain in the premises and the landlord shall be liable for all foreseeable damages shown to have been caused by his wrongful conduct. Any funds remaining in the registry of the court shall be distributed to the parties in accordance with the judgment of the court.

(c) Any writ of possession issued pursuant to this article shall authorize the removal of the tenant or his or her personal property or both from the premises and permit the placement of such personal property on some portion of the landlord's property or on other property as may be designated by the landlord and as may be approved by the executing officer; provided, however, that the landlord shall not be a bailee of such personal property and shall owe no duty to the tenant regarding such personal property. After execution of the writ, such property shall be regarded as abandoned.

§ 44-7-56. *Appeal*

Any judgment by the trial court shall be appealable pursuant to Chapters 2, 3, 6, and 7 of Title 5, provided that any such appeal shall be filed within seven days of the date such judgment was entered and provided, further, that, after the notice of appeal is filed with the clerk of the trial court, the clerk shall immediately notify the trial judge of the notice of appeal and the trial judge may, within 15 days, supplement the record with findings of fact and conclusions of law which will be considered as a part of the order of the judge in that case. If the judgment of the trial court is against the tenant and the tenant appeals this judgment, the tenant shall be required to pay into the registry of the court all sums found by the trial court to be due for rent in order to remain in possession of the premises. The tenant shall also be required to pay all future rent as it becomes due into the registry of the trial court pursuant to paragraph (1) of subsection (a) of Code Section 44-7-54 until the issue has been finally determined on appeal.

§ 44-7-57. *Applicability of article to croppers and servants after termination of employment*

This article shall apply to croppers and servants who continue to hold possession of lands and tenements after their employment as croppers or servants has terminated and in the same manner as it relates to tenants.

§ 44-7-58. *False statements*

Anyone who, under oath or affirmation, knowingly and willingly makes a false statement in an affidavit signed pursuant to Code Section 44-7-50 or in an answer filed pursuant to Code Section 44-7-51 shall be guilty of a misdemeanor.

Article 4. Distress Warrants

§ 44-7-70. Power of landlord to distrain for rent

The landlord shall have power to distrain for rent as soon as the same is due if the tenant is seeking to remove his property from the premises.

§ 44-7-71. Application for distress warrant

When rent is due or the tenant is seeking to remove his property, the landlord, his agent, his attorney in fact, or his attorney at law may, upon a statement of the facts under oath, apply for a distress warrant before the judge of the superior court, the state court, the civil court, or the magistrate court within the county where the tenant may reside or where his property may be found.

§ 44-7-72. Summons to be served on defendant; time of hearing

When the affidavit provided for in Code Section 44-7-71 is made, the judge of the superior court, the state court, the civil court, or the magistrate court before whom it was made shall grant and issue a summons to the marshal or the sheriff or his deputy of the county where the tenant resides or where his property may be found. A copy of the summons and the affidavit shall be personally served upon the defendant. If an officer is unable to serve the defendant personally, service may be given by delivering the summons and affidavit to any person who is sui juris residing on the premises. The summons served on the defendant pursuant to this Code section shall command and require the tenant to appear at a hearing on a day certain not less than five nor more than seven days from the date of actual service.

§ 44-7-73. Offer of payment by tenant

In an action for nonpayment of rent, the tenant shall be allowed to tender to the landlord, within seven days of the day the tenant was served with the summons pursuant to Code Section 44-7-72, all rents allegedly owed plus the cost of the distress warrant. Such a tender shall be a complete defense to the action.

§ 44-7-74. *Answer; distress warrant granted on failure to answer; trial*

(a) At or before the time of the hearing, the defendant may answer in writing. The defendant may answer orally at the time of the hearing. If the answer is oral, the substance thereof shall be endorsed upon the affidavit. The answer may contain any legal or equitable defense or counterclaim.

(b) If the tenant fails to answer, the court shall grant a distress warrant; and the plaintiff shall be entitled to a verdict and judgment by default for all rents due as if every item and paragraph of the affidavit provided for in Code Section 44-7-71 were supported by proper evidence, which verdict shall be in open court or chambers and without the intervention of a jury.

(c) If the tenant answers, a trial of the issues shall be had in accordance with the procedure prescribed for civil actions in courts of record except that if the action is tried in the magistrate court the trial shall be had in accordance with the procedures prescribed for that court. Every effort shall be made by the trial court to expedite a trial of the issues. The defendant shall be allowed to remain in possession of the premises and his property pending the final outcome of the litigation, provided that he complies with Code Section 44-7-75.

§ 44-7-75. *Payment of rent into court*

(a) At the time the tenant answers, the tenant shall pay into the registry of the trial court all rent admittedly owed prior to the issuance of the summons; provided, however, that, in lieu of such payment, the tenant shall be allowed to submit to the court a receipt indicating that the payment has been made to the landlord. In the event that the amount of rent is in controversy, the court shall determine the amount of rent to be paid into court in the same manner as provided in subsection (b) of this Code section.

(b) The tenant shall pay into the registry of the trial court all rent which becomes due after the issuance of the summons and shall pay said rent as it becomes due. If the landlord and tenant disagree as to the amount of rent, either or both of them may submit to the court any written rental contract for the purpose of establishing the amount of the rent to be paid into the registry of the court. If the amount of rent is in controversy and no written rental agreement exists between the tenant and the landlord, the court shall require the amount of rent to be a sum equal to the last previous rental payment made by the tenant and accepted by the landlord without written objection.

(c) If the landlord is also seeking a dispossessory warrant against the tenant pursuant to Article 3 of this chapter, money paid into court under Code Section 44-7-54 shall fully satisfy the requirements under subsections (a) and (b) of this Code section.

(d) After the date of the service of the summons as provided in Code Section 44-7-72, the tenant shall not transfer, convey, remove, or conceal his property without either posting bond as provided in Code Section 44-7-76 or complying with subsections (a) and (b) of this Code section.

(e) If the tenant shall fail to comply with any of the provisions of this Code section, the tenant shall not be entitled to retain possession of his property pending a trial on the merits as provided by Code Section 44-7-74 unless he posts bond as provided by Code Section 44-7-76. Failure to comply with any provision of this Code section shall in no way affect the tenant's ability to litigate the issues raised in his answer but shall only affect the possession of the property pendente lite. If judgment is against the tenant, the property involved shall be seized by the marshal, the sheriff, or the deputy, as the case may be, and held thereby for levy and sale after judgment as provided by Code Section 44-7-79.

(f) The court shall order the clerk of the court to pay to the landlord the amounts paid into the registry of the court as such payments are made; provided, however, that, if the tenant claims that he is entitled to all or a part of the funds and such claim is an issue of controversy in the litigation, the court shall order the clerk to pay to the landlord without delay only that portion of the funds to which the tenant has made no claim in the proceedings. That part of the funds which is a matter of controversy in the litigation shall remain in the registry of the court until a final determination of the issues.

§ 44-7-76. Bond

In all cases where the tenant may desire to transfer, remove, or convey any of his property after the service of summons, the tenant shall post bond with good security for a sum equal to the value of the property or the amount of the rent alleged to be due, whichever is less, to be estimated by the judge, for the delivery of the property at the time and place of sale if the property shall be found subject to such rent. Upon the approval of the bond by the judge, the tenant may convey, transfer, or remove his property without restriction.

§ 44-7-77. Judgment and satisfaction

(a) If, on the trial of the case, the judgment is against the tenant, the judgment shall be entered against the tenant for all rent due and for any other claim relating to the dispute and the distress warrant shall be granted.

(b) If the judgment is for the tenant, he shall be entitled to remain in the premises and in possession of his property and the landlord shall be liable for all foreseeable damages shown to have been caused by his wrongful conduct. Any funds remaining in the registry of the court shall be distributed to the parties in accordance with the judgment of the court. If the tenant has been deprived of the possession of his property pendente lite pursuant to subsection (e) of Code Section 44-7-75, the court shall order that the property be returned immediately to the tenant.

§ 44-7-78. Appeal

Any judgment by the trial court shall be appealable to the appellate court pursuant to Chapters 2, 3, 6, and 7 of Title 5. If the judgment of the trial court is against the tenant and the tenant appeals this judgment, the tenant shall remain in the premises and in possession of his property; provided, however, that the tenant shall comply with all provisions of Code Section 44-7-75 or 44-7-76 until the issue has been finally determined on appeal.

§ 44-7-79. Execution and levy

Whenever a distress warrant is granted pursuant to this article, the distress warrant may be levied by the marshal, the sheriff, or the deputy on any property belonging to said tenant whether found on the premises or elsewhere; and the marshal, the sheriff, or the deputy shall advertise and sell the property in the same manner as in the case of levy and sale under execution.

§ 44-7-80. Lien of landlord to attach from time of affidavit; priorities

The landlord's lien for his rent shall attach from the time that the affidavit is made pursuant to Code Section 44-7-71; but it shall take precedence over no lien of older date except as to the crop raised on the premises.

Appendix B

Official Code of Georgia Annotated
Title 15 – Courts
Chapter 10 – Magistrate Courts

Most dispossessory actions in Georgia take place in the Magistrate Courts of each county. The following are excerpts from the Georgia Code describing the Magistrate Courts in Georgia and the civil procedures applicable therein. If a dispossessory action takes place in the Superior Court or State Court, however, these rules will not apply; instead, the applicable procedures are found in the Georgia Civil Practice Act [O.C.G.A., Title 9] and the Uniform Rules of Superior/State Court.

Article 1. General Provisions
§ 15-10-1. *One magistrate court in each county*
§ 15-10-2. *Jurisdiction and powers*

Article 3. Civil Proceedings
§ 15-10-40. *Article to govern civil proceedings*
§ 15-10-41. *No jury trials; appeals*
§ 15-10-42. *Proceedings not subject to "Georgia Civil Practice Act"*
§ 15-10-43. *Commencement of action; service; answer*
§ 15-10-44. *Trial; dismissal; continuance*
§ 15-10-45. *Counterclaims*
§ 15-10-46. *Staying judgments and executions; partial payments*

Article 1. General Provisions

§ 15-10-1. *One magistrate court in each county*

There shall be one magistrate court in each county of the state which shall be known as the Magistrate Court of County.

§ 15-10-2. *Jurisdiction and powers*

Each magistrate court and each magistrate thereof shall have jurisdiction and power over the following matters:

...

(5) The trial of civil claims including garnishment and attachment in which exclusive jurisdiction is not vested in the superior court and the amount demanded or the value of the property claimed does not exceed $15,000.00, provided that no prejudgment attachment may be granted;

(6) The issuance of summons, trial of issues, and issuance of writs and judgments in dispossessory proceedings and distress warrant proceedings as provided in Articles 3 and 4 of Chapter 7 of Title 44;

...

Article 3. Civil Proceedings

§ 15-10-40. *Article to govern civil proceedings*

This article shall govern civil proceedings in the magistrate court.

§ 15-10-41. No jury trials; appeals

(a) There shall be no jury trials in the magistrate court.

(b)

   (1) Except as otherwise provided in this subsection, appeals may be had from judgments returned in the magistrate court to the state court of the county or to the superior court of the county and the same provisions now provided for by general law for appeals contained in Article 2 of Chapter 3 of Title 5 shall be applicable to appeals from the magistrate court, the same to be a de novo appeal. The provisions of said Article 2 of Chapter 3 of Title 5 shall also apply to appeals to state court.

   (2) No appeal shall lie from a default judgment or from a dismissal for want of prosecution after a nonappearance of a plaintiff for trial. Any voluntary dismissal by the plaintiff or by order of the court for want of prosecution shall be without prejudice except that the filing of a second such dismissal shall operate as an adjudication upon the merits. Review, including review of a denial of a postjudgment motion to vacate a judgment, shall be by certiorari to the state court of that county or to the superior court of that county.

§ 15-10-42. Proceedings not subject to "Georgia Civil Practice Act"

Proceedings in the magistrate court shall not be subject to Chapter 11 of Title 9, the "Georgia Civil Practice Act."

§ 15-10-43. Commencement of action; service; answer

(a) Actions shall be commenced by the filing of a statement of claim, including the last known address of the defendant, in concise form and free from technicalities. The plaintiff or his or her agent shall sign and verify the statement of claim by oath or affirmation. At the request of any individual, the judge or clerk may prepare the statement of claim and other papers required to be filed in an action. The statement of claim shall include a brief statement of the claim giving the defendant reasonable notice of the basis for each claim contained in the statement of claim and the address at which the plaintiff desires to receive the notice of hearing.

(b) A copy of the verified statement of claim shall be served on the defendant personally, or by leaving a copy thereof at the defendant's dwelling or usual place of abode with some person of suitable age and discretion then residing therein, or by delivering a copy of the claim to an agent authorized by appointment or by law to receive service of process, and such service shall be sufficient. Service of said process shall be made within the county as provided in this Code section. Service outside the county shall be by second original as provided in Code Section 9-10-72. Said service shall be made by any official or person authorized by law to serve process in the superior court, by a constable, or by any person sui juris who is not a party to, or otherwise interested in, the action, who is specially appointed by the judge of said court for that purpose. When the claim and notice are served by a private individual, such individual shall make proof of service by affidavit, showing the time and place of such service on the defendant.

(c) An answer to the claim must be filed with the court or orally presented to the judge or clerk of the court within 30 days after service of the statement of claim on the defendant to avoid a default. The answer shall be in concise form and free from technical requirements, but must admit or deny the claim of the plaintiff. The answer shall contain the address at which the defendant desires to receive the notice of hearing. If the answer is presented to the judge or clerk orally, the judge or clerk shall reduce the answer to writing. A copy of the answer shall be forwarded to the plaintiff and defendant with the notice of hearing. If an answer is timely filed or presented, the court shall within ten days of filing or presentation of the answer notify the defendant and the plaintiff of the calling of a hearing on the claim. The notice shall include the date, hour, and location of the hearing, which date shall be not less than 15 nor more than 30 days after the date the notice is given. The notice shall be served on the plaintiff and the defendant by mail or personal service to the address given by the plaintiff at the time he or she files his or her claim and the address given by the defendant at the time he or she files or presents his or her answer. The date of mailing shall be the date the notice is given. The clerk shall enter a certificate of service.

(d) Upon failure of the defendant to answer the claim within 30 days after service of the statement of claim, the defendant shall be in default. The defaulting party may open the default upon filing an answer and upon payment of costs within 15 days of default. If the defendant is still in default after the expiration of 15 days after the answer is due, the plaintiff shall be entitled to a default judgment without further proof if the claim is for liquidated damages. When the claim is for unliquidated damages, the plaintiff must offer proof of the damage amount. Separate notice of the date and time of the unliquidated damages hearing shall be sent to the defendant at his or her service address. The defendant shall be allowed to submit evidence at that hearing on the issue of the amount of damage only.

(e)

(1) When a hearing is scheduled pursuant to subsection (c) of this Code section, upon failure of the defendant to appear for the hearing, the plaintiff shall be entitled to have the defendant's answer stricken and a default judgment entered; provided, however, that no default judgment shall be granted if the defendant appears at trial through counsel. If the claim is for liquidated damages, the plaintiff shall be entitled to take a judgment in the amount set forth in the complaint without further proof. If the claim is for unliquidated damages, the plaintiff shall proceed to prove his or her damages and take judgment in an amount determined by the judge.

(2) When a hearing is scheduled pursuant to subsection (d) of this Code section, upon failure of the defendant to appear, the plaintiff shall be entitled to submit proof of the damages and take judgment in anamount determined by the judge.

(3) If the plaintiff fails to appear for a hearing scheduled pursuant to either subsection (c) or (d) of this Code section, the court on motion of the defendant, or on its own motion, may dismiss the plaintiff's complaint, with or without prejudice, in the discretion of the court.

(f) At any time before final judgment, the court, in its discretion, upon payment of costs, may allow the default to be opened for providential cause preventing the filing of required pleadings or for excusable neglect or where the judge, from all the facts, shall determine that a proper case has been made for the default to be opened, on terms to be fixed by the court. In order to allow the default to be thus opened, the showing shall be made under oath, shall set up a meritorious defense, shall offer to plead instanter, and shall announce ready to proceed with the trial.

(g) Notwithstanding the provisions of Code Section 15-10-42, the magistrate court may grant relief from a judgment under the same circumstances as the state court may grant such relief. Requests for relief from judgments pursuant to this Code section in the magistrate court shall be by filing a written motion which sets forth the issues with reasonable specificity. The procedure shall then be the same as in other cases except the court may assess costs as seem just.

(h) A complaint in equity to set aside a judgment of the magistrate court may be brought under the same circumstances as a complaint to set aside a judgment in a court of record.

(i) Nothing in this chapter shall be construed to prohibit an employee of any corporation or other legal entity from representing the corporation or legal entity before the magistrate court.

§ 15-10-44. Trial; dismissal; continuance

(a) The trial shall be conducted on the day set for the hearing, or at such later time as the judge may set. Immediately prior to the trial of any case, the judge shall counsel the parties to make an earnest effort to settle the controversy by conciliation. If the parties fail to settle their differences without a trial, the judge shall proceed with the hearing on its merits.

(b) The judge shall conduct the trial in such manner as to do substantial justice between the parties according to the rules of substantive law. All rules and regulations relating to pleading, practice, and procedure shall be liberally construed so as to administer justice.

(c) If the plaintiff fails to appear, the action may be dismissed for want of prosecution, the defendant may proceed to a trial on the merits, or the case may be continued as the judge may direct. If both parties fail to appear, the judge may continue the case, order the same dismissed for want of prosecution, or make any other just and proper disposition thereof, as justice may require.

§ 15-10-45. Counterclaims

(a) If any defendant has a claim against the plaintiff arising out of the transaction or occurrence that is the subject matter of the plaintiff's claim, which claim does not require for its adjudication the presence of third parties over whom the court cannot obtain jurisdiction, such claim must be asserted by the defendant at or before the hearing on plaintiff's claim or thereafter be barred.

(b) If any defendant has a claim against the plaintiff other than a compulsory counterclaim described in subsection (a) of this Code section, such claim may be asserted by the defendant at or before the hearing on the plaintiff's claim.

(c) If any defendant asserts a claim against the plaintiff, the defendant shall file with the court a statement of the claim in concise form and free from technicalities. The defendant's claim shall give the plaintiff reasonable notice of the basis for each claim contained in the statement of claim. The defendant shall sign and verify the statement of claim by oath or affirmation. At the request of a defendant, the judge or clerk may prepare the statement.

(d) If the amount of a counterclaim exceeds the jurisdictional limits of the magistrate court, the case shall be transferred to any court of the county which has jurisdictional limits which exceed the amount of the counterclaim. If there is more than one court to which the action may be transferred, the parties may agree on the court to which the action shall be transferred, and, in the absence of any agreement, the judge of the magistrate court shall determine the court to which the action shall be transferred. If there is no other court to which the action may be transferred, it shall be transferred to the superior court of the county.

(e) A counterclaim may in the discretion of the magistrate be tried either separately or jointly with the plaintiff's claim.

§ 15-10-46. *Staying judgments and executions; partial payments*

(a) When the judgment is to be rendered and the party against whom it is to be entered requests it, the judge shall inquire fully into the earnings and financial status of such party and shall have full discretionary power to stay the entry of judgment, to stay execution, and to order partial payments in such amounts, over such periods, and upon such terms as seem just under the circumstances and as will assure a definite and steady reduction of the judgment until it is fully and completely satisfied.

(b) The judge of the magistrate court shall not be obligated to collect such deferred partial payments on judgments so rendered but, if the plaintiff so requests, he may do so at the expense of the plaintiff for clerical and accounting costs incurred thereby, not to exceed 10 percent of each payment.

§ 15-10-47. Money judgments

(a) Except where otherwise provided by law, the general laws and rules applicable to the effect, recordation, execution, and enforcement of money judgments in civil cases in the superior courts of this state shall be applicable to and govern the magistrate courts.

(b) Upon the issuance of any execution by the magistrate court, the clerk of the magistrate court shall immediately transmit a copy of the execution to the clerk of superior court of the county. The fee of the clerk of superior court for recording the execution on the general execution docket shall be charged and collected by the magistrate court contemporaneously with or prior to the issuance of the execution but not before the entry of judgment in the action; and such fee shall be transmitted by the clerk of magistrate court to the clerk of superior court together with the copy of the execution. The clerk of the superior court shall immediately enter the execution upon the general execution docket in the same manner as executions issued by the superior court, without the necessity of any action by the plaintiff in fi. fa.

§ 15-10-49. Procedure in ... dispossessory proceedings

...

(c) Procedure in dispossessory proceedings and in distress warrant proceedings shall be subject to Articles 3 and 4 of Chapter 7 of Title 44.

§ 15-10-50. Post-judgment interrogatories in aid of judgments

(a) In aid of any judgment or execution issued by any court in this state upon which the unpaid balance does not exceed the jurisdictional amount for civil claims in magistrate court as provided in paragraph (5) of Code Section 15-10-2, the judgment creditor or his successor in interest when that interest appears of record, may, in addition to any other process or remedy provided by law, examine the judgment debtor by propounding the interrogatories specified in this Code section in the manner provided in this Code section.

(b) If the judgment or execution concerning which interrogatories are being propounded was issued by the magistrate court, the judgment creditor may, after the entry of judgment, file the form interrogatories specified in this Code section with the clerk of the same magistrate court, along with costs of $10.00. Interrogatories filed under this subsection shall be served upon the judgment debtor by certified mail or statutory overnight delivery.

(c) Interrogatories propounded pursuant to a judgment entered in any other court shall be filed as a new civil action and shall be accompanied by the filing and service fees required for civil actions in that magistrate court. Interrogatories propounded under this subsection shall be served upon the judgment debtor in the manner provided for service of process in civil actions in magistrate court.

(d) The interrogatories, verification, and notice shall be in substantially the following form: [omitted; see Appendix D]

(e) The court in its discretion may limit the number of times interrogatories may be propounded upon a judgment debtor, may relieve a judgment debtor of the obligation to answer one or more propounded interrogatories, and may for good cause shown enlarge the time for answering any interrogatory. The court may if necessary compel the answering of interrogatories, but the sanction of contempt shall be applied only after notice and an opportunity for hearing and a showing of willful failure to answer or willful failure to answer fully and truthfully.

(f) An evasive or incomplete answer to an interrogatory shall be treated as a failure to answer.

(g) Notwithstanding the provisions of Code Section 15-10-42, the judgment creditor or a successor in interest when that interest appears of record may, in addition to any other process or remedy provided by law, utilize the discovery provisions set forth in Code Section 9-11-69.

§ 15-10-51. *Clerk or deputy clerk may be authorized to sign notice or summons in pending civil actions*

The chief magistrate of each county may, by local rule of court, authorize the clerk of the magistrate court or one or more deputy clerks of the court to sign any notice or summons in any civil action pending in the court.

§ 15-10-52. *Action by assignee of obligee to show action in name of original obligee by assignee*

The style of any action, other than a proceeding brought pursuant to Chapter 7 of Title 44, relating to landlord and tenant, brought in the magistrate court by the assignee of the obligee of any obligation shall show the action in the name of the original obligee by the assignee.

§ 15-10-53. *Filing by electronic means; electronic signature and verification; service; challenge to authenticity; fees*

(a) Any magistrate court may provide for the filing of civil, garnishment, distress warrant, dispossessory, foreclosure, abandoned motor vehicle, and all other noncriminal actions, claims, answers, counterclaims, pleadings, postjudgment interrogatories, and other documents by electronic means.

(b) Any pleading or document filed electronically shall be in a format prescribed by the court.

(c) Any pleading or document filed electronically shall include the electronic signature of the person filing the pleading or document as defined in Code Section 10-12-2.

(d) Any pleading or document filed electronically which is required to be verified, verified under oath, or be accompanied by an affidavit may include such verification, oath, or affidavit by one of the following methods:

(1) As provided in Code Section 10-12-11;

(2) By oath or affirmation of the party filing the pleading at the time of the trial of the case;

(3) By supplemental verified pleading; or

(4) By electronic verification, oath, or affidavit in substantially the following form:

"By affixing this electronic verification, oath, or affidavit to the pleading(s) submitted to the court and attaching my electronic signature hereon, I do hereby swear or affirm that the statements set forth in the above pleading(s) are true and correct. Date: _____ Electronic Signature: _____"

(e) Service of any claim or complaint filed electronically shall be made as provided by law. Service of all subsequent pleadings and notices may be made electronically only on a party who has filed pleadings electronically; service on all other parties shall be made by such other means as are provided by law. Each pleading or document which is required to be served on other parties shall include a certificate of service indicating the method by which service on the other party has been made. An electronic certificate of service shall be made in substantially the following form:

"By affixing this electronic certificate of service to the pleading(s) or document(s) submitted to the court and attaching my electronic signature hereon, I do hereby swear or affirm that I have this date served the opposing party with a copy of this pleading by e-mail or placing a copy in regular mail with sufficient postage thereon to the following address: (set forth address of opposing party). Date: _____ Electronic Signature: _____"

(f) Nothing in this Code section shall prevent a party from contesting an electronic pleading, document, or signature on the basis of forgery or fraud. Any pleading or document found by the court to have been fraudulently filed shall be stricken from the record.

(g) Where the authenticity or the integrity of an electronic pleading, document, or signature is challenged, the proponent of the electronic pleading, document, or signature shall have the burden of proving that the electronic pleading, document, or signature is authentic.

(h) Upon the receipt of any pleading or other document filed electronically, the clerk of magistrate court shall notify the filer of receipt of the pleading or document. Such notice shall include the date and time the court accepted the pleading or document as filed.

(i) Any pleading or document filed electronically shall be deemed filed as of the time the clerk of court gains electronic control of the document.

(j) When the filing of the pleading or document requires the payment of a fee, the clerk of magistrate court may establish procedures for the payment of such fees connected with such filing. The filing of any such pleading or document shall create an obligation by the party to pay such fee to the clerk of court instanter.

(k) The clerk of court may assess an additional transaction fee or fees for each electronic filing and electronic payment.

Appendix C

Title III – Rent, Installment Contracts, Mortgages, Liens, Assignment, Leases

Title VIII – Civil Liability

§ 501. Short title [Sec. 1]

This Act [50 U.S.C. App. §§ 501 et seq.] may be cited as the Servicemembers Civil Relief Act.

§ 502. Purpose [Sec. 2]

The purposes of this Act are—

    (1) to provide for, strengthen, and expedite the national defense through protection extended by this Act to servicemembers of the United States to enable such persons to devote their entire energy to the defense needs of the Nation; and

    (2) to provide for the temporary suspension of judicial and administrative proceedings and transactions that may adversely affect the civil rights of service-

members during their military service.

Title I – General Provisions
§ 511. Definitions [Sec. 101]

For the purposes of this Act:

(1) Servicemember. The term "servicemember" means a member of the uniformed services, as that term is defined in section 101(a)(5) of title 10, United States Code.

(2) Military service. The term "military service" means—

(A) in the case of a servicemember who is a member of the Army, Navy, Air Force, Marine Corps, or Coast Guard—

(i) active duty, as defined in section 101(d)(1) of title 10, United States Code, and

(ii) in the case of a member of the National Guard, includes service under a call to active service authorized by the President or the Secretary of Defense for a period of more than 30 consecutive days under section 502(f) of title 32, United States Code, for purposes of responding to a national emergency declared by the President and supported by Federal funds;

(B) in the case of a servicemember who is a commissioned officer of the Public Health Service or the National Oceanic and Atmospheric Administration, active service; and

(C) any period during which a servicemember is absent from duty on account of sickness, wounds, leave, or other lawful cause.

(3) Period of military service. The term "period of military service" means the period beginning on the date on which a servicemember enters military service and ending on the date on which the servicemember is released from military service or dies while in military service.

(4) Dependent. The term "dependent", with respect to a servicemember, means—

(A) the servicemember's spouse;

(B) the servicemember's child (as defined in section 101(4) of title 38, United States Code); or

(C) an individual for whom the servicemember provided more than one-half of the individual's support for 180 days immediately preceding an application for relief under this Act [sections 501 to 596 of this Appendix].

(5) Court. The term "court" means a court or an administrative agency of the United States or of any State (including any political subdivision of a State), whether or not a court or administrative agency of record.

(6) State. The term "State" includes—

(A) a commonwealth, territory, or possession of the United States; and

(B) the District of Columbia.

(7) Secretary concerned. The term "Secretary concerned"—

(A) with respect to a member of the armed forces, has the meaning given that term in section 101(a)(9) of title 10, United States Code;

(B) with respect to a commissioned officer of the Public Health Service, means the Secretary of Health and Human Services; and

(C) with respect to a commissioned officer of the National Oceanic and Atmospheric Administration, means the Secretary of Commerce.

...

(9) Judgment. The term 'judgment' means any judgment, decree, order, or ruling, final or temporary.

§ 512. *Jurisdiction and applicability of Act [Sec. 102]*

(a) Jurisdiction

This Act applies to—

(1) the United States;

(2) each of the States, including the political subdivisions thereof; and

(3) all territory subject to the jurisdiction of the United States.

(b) Applicability to proceedings

This Act applies to any judicial or administrative proceeding commenced in any court or agency in any jurisdiction subject to this Act. This Act does not apply to criminal proceedings.

(c) Court in which application may be made

When under this Act any application is required to be made to a court in which no proceeding has already been commenced with respect to the matter, such application may be made to any court which would otherwise have jurisdiction over the matter.

§ 513. *Protection of persons secondarily liable [Sec. 103]*

(a) Extension of protection when actions stayed, postponed, or suspended. Whenever pursuant to this Act a court stays, postpones, or suspends (1) the enforcement of an obligation or liability, (2) the prosecution of a suit or proceeding, (3) the entry or enforcement of an order, writ, judgment, or decree, or (4) the performance of any other act, the court may likewise grant such a stay, postponement, or suspension to a surety, guarantor, endorser, accommodation maker, comaker, or other person who is or may be primarily or secondarily subject to the obligation or liability the performance or enforcement of which is stayed, postponed, or suspended.

(b) Vacation or set-aside of judgments. When a judgment or decree is vacated or set aside, in whole or in part, pursuant to this Act, the court may also set aside or vacate, as the case may be, the judgment or decree as to a surety, guarantor, endorser, accommodation maker, comaker, or other person who is or may be primarily or secondarily liable on the contract or liability for the enforcement of the judgment or decree.

(c) Bail bond not to be enforced during period of military service. A court may not enforce a bail bond during the period of military service of the principal on the bond when military service prevents the surety from obtaining the attendance of the principal. The court may discharge the surety and exonerate the bail, in accordance with principles of equity and justice, during or after the period of military service of the principal.

(d) Waiver of rights.

    (1) Waivers not precluded. This Act does not prevent a waiver in writing by a surety, guarantor, endorser, accommodation maker, comaker, or other person (whether primarily or secondarily liable on an obligation or liability) of the protections provided under subsections (a) and (b). Any such waiver is effective only if it is executed as an instrument separate from the obligation or liability with respect to which it applies.

    (2) Waiver invalidated upon entrance to military service. If a waiver under paragraph (1) is executed by an individual who after the execution of the waiver enters military service, or by a dependent of an individual who after the execution of the waiver enters military service, the waiver is not valid after the beginning of the period of such military service unless the waiver was executed by such individual or dependent during the period specified in section [50 U.S.C. App. § 516].

§ 514. *Extension of protections to citizens serving with allied forces* [Sec. 104]

A citizen of the United States who is serving with the forces of a nation with which the United States is allied in the prosecution of a war or military action is entitled to the relief and protections provided under this Act if that service with the allied force is similar to military service as defined in this Act. The relief and protections provided to such citizen shall terminate on the date of discharge or release from such service.

§ 516. *Extension of rights and protections to reserves ordered to report for military service and to persons ordered to report for induction [Sec. 106]*

(a) Reserves ordered to report for military service. A member of a reserve component who is ordered to report for military service is entitled to the rights and protections of this title and titles II and III during the period beginning on the date of the member's receipt of the order and ending on the date on which the member reports for military service (or, if the order is revoked before the member so reports, or the date on which the order is revoked).

(b) Persons ordered to report for induction. A person who has been ordered to report for induction under the Military Selective Service Act (50 U.S.C. App. §§ 451 et seq.) is entitled to the rights and protections provided a servicemember under this title and titles II and III during the period beginning on the date of receipt of the order for induction and ending on the date on which the person reports for induction (or, if the order to report for induction is revoked before the date on which the person reports for induction, on the date on which the order is revoked).

§ 517. *Waiver of rights pursuant to written agreement [Sec. 107]*

(a) In general. A servicemember may waive any of the rights and protections provided by this Act. Any such waiver that applies to an action listed in subsection (b) of this section is effective only if it is in writing and is executed as an instrument separate from the obligation or liability to which it applies. In the case of a waiver that permits an action described in subsection (b), the waiver is effective only if made pursuant to a written agreement of the parties that is executed during or after the servicemember's period of military service. The written agreement shall specify the legal instrument to which the waiver applies and, if the servicemember is not a party to that instrument, the servicemember concerned.

(b) Actions requiring waivers in writing. The requirement in subsection (a) for a written waiver applies to the following:

(1) The modification, termination, or cancellation of—
(A) a contract, lease, or bailment; or
(B) an obligation secured by a mortgage, trust, deed, lien, or other security in the nature of a mortgage.

(2) The repossession, retention, foreclosure, sale, forfeiture, or taking possession of property that—
(A) is security for any obligation; or
(B) was purchased or received under a contract, lease, or bailment.

(c) Prominent Display of Certain Contract Rights Waivers. Any waiver in writing of a right or protection provided by this Act that applies to a contract, lease, or similar legal instrument must be in at least 12 point type.

(d) Coverage of periods after orders received. For the purposes of this section—

(1) a person to whom section 106 [50 U.S.C. App. § 516] applies shall be considered to be a servicemember; and

(2) the period with respect to such a person specified in subsection (a) or (b), as the case may be, of section 106 [50 U.S.C. App. § 516] shall be considered to be a period of military service.

§ 518. *Exercise of rights under Act not to affect certain future financial transactions [Sec. 108]*

Application by a servicemember for, or receipt by a servicemember of, a stay, postponement, or suspension pursuant to this Act in the payment of a tax, fine, penalty, insurance premium, or other civil obligation or liability of that servicemember shall not itself (without regard to other considerations) provide the basis for any of the following:

(1) A determination by a lender or other person that the servicemember is unable to pay the civil obligation or liability in accordance with its terms.

§ 519. Legal representatives [Sec. 109]

(a) Representative. A legal representative of a servicemember for purposes of this Act is either of the following:

  (1) An attorney acting on the behalf of a servicemember.

  (2) An individual possessing a power of attorney.

(b) Application. Whenever the term "servicemember" is used in this Act, such term shall be treated as including a reference to a legal representative of the servicemember.

Title II – General Relief

§ 521. Protection of servicemembers against default judgments [Sec. 201]

(a) Applicability of section. This section applies to any civil action or proceeding, including any child custody proceeding, in which the defendant does not make an appearance.

(b) Affidavit requirement

  (1) Plaintiff to file affidavit. In any action or proceeding covered by this section, the court, before entering judgment for the plaintiff, shall require the plaintiff to file with the court an affidavit—

    (A) stating whether or not the defendant is in military service and showing necessary facts to support the affidavit; or

    (B) if the plaintiff is unable to determine whether or not the defendant is in military service, stating that the plaintiff is unable to determine whether or not the defendant is in military service.

  (2) Appointment of attorney to represent defendant in military service. If in an action covered by this section it appears that the defendant is in military service, the court may not enter a judgment until after the court appoints an attorney to represent the defendant. If an attorney appointed under this sec-

tion to represent a servicemember cannot locate the servicemember, actions by the attorney in the case shall not waive any defense of the servicemember or otherwise bind the servicemember.

(3) Defendant's military status not ascertained by affidavit. If based upon the affidavits filed in such an action, the court is unable to determine whether the defendant is in military service, the court, before entering judgment, may require the plaintiff to file a bond in an amount approved by the court. If the defendant is later found to be in military service, the bond shall be available to indemnify the defendant against any loss or damage the defendant may suffer by reason of any judgment for the plaintiff against the defendant, should the judgment be set aside in whole or in part. The bond shall remain in effect until expiration of the time for appeal and setting aside of a judgment under applicable Federal or State law or regulation or under any applicable ordinance of a political subdivision of a State. The court may issue such orders or enter such judgments as the court determines necessary to protect the rights of the defendant under this Act.

(4) Satisfaction of requirement for affidavit. The requirement for an affidavit under paragraph (1) may be satisfied by a statement, declaration, verification, or certificate, in writing, subscribed and certified or declared to be true under penalty of perjury.

(c) Penalty for making or using false affidavit. A person who makes or uses an affidavit permitted under subsection (b) (or a statement, declaration, verification, or certificate as authorized under subsection (b)(4)) knowing it to be false, shall be fined as provided in title 18, United States Code, or imprisoned for not more than one year, or both.

(d) Stay of proceedings. In an action covered by this section in which the defendant is in military service, the court shall grant a stay of proceedings for a minimum period of 90 days under this subsection upon application of counsel, or on the court's own motion, if the court determines that–

(1) there may be a defense to the action and a defense cannot be presented without the presence of the defendant; or

(2) after due diligence, counsel has been unable to contact the defendant or otherwise determine if a meritorious defense exists.

(e) Inapplicability of section 202 procedures. A stay of proceedings under subsection (d) shall not be controlled by procedures or requirements under section 202 [50 U.S.C. App. § 522].

(f) Section 202 protection. If a servicemember who is a defendant in an action covered by this section receives actual notice of the action, the servicemember may request a stay of proceeding under section 202 [50 U.S.C. App. § 522].

(g) Vacation or setting aside of default judgments.

(1) Authority for court to vacate or set aside judgment. If a default judgment is entered in an action covered by this section against a servicemember during the servicemember's period of military service (or within 60 days after termination of or release from such military service), the court entering the judgment shall, upon application by or on behalf of the servicemember, reopen the judgment for the purpose of allowing the servicemember to defend the action if it appears that—

(A) the servicemember was materially affected by reason of that military service in making a defense to the action; and

(B) the servicemember has a meritorious or legal defense to the action or some part of it.

(2) Time for filing application. An application under this subsection must be filed not later than 90 days after the date of the termination of or release from

military service.

    (h) Protection of bona fide purchaser. If a court vacates, sets aside, or reverses a default judgment against a servicemember and the vacating, setting aside, or reversing is because of a provision of this Act, that action shall not impair a right or title acquired by a bona fide purchaser for value under the default judgment.

§ 522. *Stay of proceedings when servicemember has notice [Sec. 202]*

    ...

    (f) Inapplicability to section 301 [50 U.S.C. App. § 531]. The protections of this section do not apply to section 301 [50 U.S.C. App. § 531].

§ 523. *Fines and penalties under contracts[Sec. 203]*

    (a) Prohibition of penalties. When an action for compliance with the terms of a contract is stayed pursuant to this Act, a penalty shall not accrue for failure to comply with the terms of the contract during the period of the stay.

    (b) Reduction or waiver of fines or penalties. If a servicemember fails to perform an obligation arising under a contract and a penalty is incurred arising from that non-performance, a court may reduce or waive the fine or penalty if—

        (1) the servicemember was in military service at the time the fine or penalty was incurred; and

        (2) the ability of the servicemember to perform the obligation was materially affected by such military service.

§ 524. *Stay or vacation of execution of judgments, attachments, and garnishments [Sec. 204]*

    (a) Court action upon material affect determination. If a servicemember, in the opinion of the court, is materially affected by reason of military service in complying with a court judgment or order, the court may on its own motion and shall on application by the servicemember—

        (1) stay the execution of any judgment or order entered against the servicemember;

...

(b) Applicability. This section applies to an action or proceeding commenced in a court against a servicemember before or during the period of the servicemember's military service or within 90 days after such service terminates.

§ 525. *Duration and term of stays; codefendants not in service [Sec. 205]*

(a) Period of stay. A stay of an action, proceeding, attachment, or execution made pursuant to the provisions of this Act by a court may be ordered for the period of military service and 90 days thereafter, or for any part of that period. The court may set the terms and amounts for such installment payments as is considered reasonable by the court.

(b) Codefendants. If the servicemember is a codefendant with others who are not in military service and who are not entitled to the relief and protections provided under this Act, the plaintiff may proceed against those other defendants with the approval of the court.

(c) Inapplicability of section. This section does not apply to sections 202 and 701 [50 U.S.C. App. §§ 522 and 591].

§ 527. *Maximum rate of interest on debts incurred before military service [Sec. 207]*

(a) Interest rate limitation.

(1) Limitation to 6 percent. An obligation or liability bearing interest at a rate in excess of 6 percent per year that is incurred by a servicemember, or the servicemember and the servicemember's spouse jointly, before the servicemember enters military service shall not bear interest at a rate in excess of 6 percent

–

(A) during the period of military service and one year thereafter, in the case of an obligation or liability consisting of a mortgage, trust deed, or other security in the nature of a mortgage; or

(B) during the period of military service, in the case of any other obligation or liability.

(2) Forgiveness of interest in excess of 6 percent. Interest at a rate in excess of 6 percent per year that would otherwise be incurred but for the prohibition in paragraph (1) is forgiven.

(3) Prevention of acceleration of principal. The amount of any periodic payment due from a servicemember under the terms of the instrument that created an obligation or liability covered by this section shall be reduced by the amount of the interest forgiven under paragraph (2) that is allocable to the period for which such payment is made.

(b) Implementation of limitation.

(1) Written notice to creditor. In order for an obligation or liability of a servicemember to be subject to the interest rate limitation in subsection (a), the servicemember shall provide to the creditor written notice and a copy of the military orders calling the servicemember to military service and any orders further extending military service, not later than 180 days after the date of the servicemember's termination or release from military service.

(2) Limitation effective as of date of order to active duty. Upon receipt of written notice and a copy of orders calling a servicemember to military service, the creditor shall treat the debt in accordance with subsection (a), effective as of the date on which the servicemember is called to military service.

(c) Creditor protection. A court may grant a creditor relief from the limitations of this section if, in the opinion of the court, the ability of the servicemember to pay interest upon the obligation or liability at a rate in excess of 6 percent per year is not materially affected by reason of the servicemember's military service.

(d) Definitions. In this section:

(1) Interest. The term "interest" includes service

charges, renewal charges, fees, or any other charges (except bona fide insurance) with respect to an obligation or liability.

(2) Obligation or liability. The term "obligation or liability" includes an obligation or liability consisting of a mortgage, trust deed, or other security in the nature of a mortgage.

(e) Penalty. Whoever knowingly violates subsection (a) shall be fined as provided in title 18, United States Code, imprisoned for not more than one year, or both.

Title III – Rent, Installment Contracts, Mortgages, Liens, Assignment, Leases

§ 531. *Evictions and distress [Sec. 301]*

(a) Court-ordered eviction.

(1) In general. Except by court order, a landlord (or another person with paramount title) may not—

(A) evict a servicemember, or the dependents of a servicemember, during a period of military service of the servicemember, from premises—

(i) that are occupied or intended to be occupied primarily as a residence; and

(ii) for which the monthly rent does not exceed $2,400, as adjusted under paragraph (2) for years after 2003; or

(B) subject such premises to a distress during the period of military service.

(2) Housing price inflation adjustment

(A) For calendar years beginning with 2004, the amount in effect under paragraph (1)(A)(ii) shall be increased by the housing price inflation adjustment for the calendar year involved.

(B) For purposes of this paragraph—

(i) The housing price inflation adjustment for any calendar year is the percentage change (if any) by which –

(I) the CPI housing component for November of the preceding calendar year, exceeds'

            (II) the CPI housing component for November of 1984.

        (ii) The term "CPI housing component" means the index published by the Bureau of Labor Statistics of the Department of Labor known as the Consumer Price Index, All Urban Consumers, Rent of Primary Residence, U.S. City Average.

    (3) Publication of housing price inflation adjustment. The Secretary of Defense shall cause to be published in the Federal Register each year the amount in effect under paragraph (1)(A)(ii) for that year following the housing price inflation adjustment for that year pursuant to paragraph (2). Such publication shall be made for a year not later than 60 days after such adjustment is made for that year.

(b) Stay of execution.

    (1) Court authority. Upon an application for eviction or distress with respect to premises covered by this section, the court may on its own motion and shall, if a request is made by or on behalf of a servicemember whose ability to pay the agreed rent is materially affected by military service –

        (A) stay the proceedings for a period of 90 days, unless in the opinion of the court, justice and equity require a longer or shorter period of time; or

        (B) adjust the obligation under the lease to preserve the interests of all parties.

    (2) Relief to landlord. If a stay is granted under paragraph (1), the court may grant to the landlord (or other person with paramount title) such relief as equity may require.

(c) Misdemeanor. Except as provided in subsection (a), a person who knowingly takes part in an eviction or distress described in subsection (a), or who knowingly attempts to do so, shall be fined as provided in title 18, United States Code, or imprisoned for not more than one year, or both.

(d) Rent allotment from pay of servicemember. To the extent required by a court order related to property which is the subject of a court action under this section, the Secretary concerned shall make an allotment from the pay of a servicemember to satisfy the terms of such order, except that any such allotment shall be subject to regulations prescribed by the Secretary concerned establishing the maximum amount of pay of servicemembers that may be allotted under this subsection.

(e) Limitation of applicability. Section 202 [50 U.S.C. § 522] is not applicable to this section.

§ 532. *Protection under installment contracts for purchase or lease [Sec. 302]*

(a) Protection upon breach of contract.

(1) Protection after entering military service. After a servicemember enters military service, a contract by the servicemember for—

...

(B) the lease or bailment of such property, may not be rescinded or terminated for a breach of terms of the contract occurring before or during that person's military service, nor may the property be repossessed for such breach without a court order.

(2) Applicability. This section applies only to a contract for which a deposit or installment has been paid by the servicemember before the servicemember enters military service.

(b) Misdemeanor. A person who knowingly resumes possession of property in violation of subsection (a), or in violation of section 107 of this Act [50 U.S.C. App. § 517], or who knowingly attempts to do so, shall be fined as provided in title 18, United States Code, or imprisoned for not more than one year, or both.

(c) Authority of court. In a hearing based on this section, the court–

(1) may order repayment to the servicemember of all or part of the prior installments or deposits as a condition of terminating the contract and resuming possession of the property;

(2) may, on its own motion, and shall on application by a servicemember when the servicemember's ability to comply with the contract is materially affected by military service, stay the proceedings for a period of time as, in the opinion of the court, justice and equity require; or

(3) may make other disposition as is equitable to preserve the interests of all parties.

§ 535. *Termination of residential or motor vehicle leases [Sec. 305]*

(a) Termination by lessee.

(1) In general. The lessee on a lease described in subsection (b) may, at the lessee's option, terminate the lease at any time after –

(a) the lessee's entry into military service; or

(b) the date of the lessee's military orders described in paragraph (1)(B) of (2)(B) of subsection (b), as the case may be.

(2) Joint leases. A lessee's termination of a lease pursuant to this subsection shall terminate any obligation a dependent of the lessee may have under the lease.

(b) Covered leases. This section applies to the following leases:

(1) Leases of premises. A lease of premises occupied, or intended to be occupied, by a servicemember or a servicemember's dependents for a residential, professional, business, agricultural, or similar purpose if—

(A) the lease is executed by or on behalf of a person who thereafter and during the term of the lease enters military service; or

(B) the servicemember, while in military service, executes the lease and thereafter receives military orders for a permanent change of station or to deploy with a military unit or as an individual in support of a military operation for a period of not less than 90 days.

...

(c) Manner of termination.

(1) In general. Termination of a lease under subsection (a) is made —

(A) by delivery by the lessee of written notice of such termination, and a copy of the servicemember's military orders, to the lessor (or the lessor's grantee), or to the lessor's agent (or the agent's grantee); and

(B) in the case of a lease of a motor vehicle, by return of the motor vehicle by the lessee to the lessor (or the lessor's grantee), or to the lessor's agent (or the agent's grantee), not later than 15 days after the date of the delivery of written notice under subparagraph (A).

(2) Delivery of notice. Delivery of notice under paragraph (1)(A) may be accomplished —

(A) by hand delivery;

(B) by private business carrier; or

(C) by placing the written notice in an envelope with sufficient postage and with return receipt requested, and addressed as designated by the lessor (or the lessor's grantee) or to the lessor's agent (or the agent's grantee), and depositing the written notice in the United States mails.

(d) Effective date of lease termination.

(1) Leases of premises. In the case of a lease described in subsection (b)(1) that provides for monthly payment of rent, termination of the lease under subsection (a) is effective 30 days after the first date on which the next rental payment is due and payable after the date on which the notice under subsection (c) is delivered. In the case of any other lease described in subsection (b)(1), termination of the lease under subsection (a) is effective on the last day of

the month following the month in which the notice is delivered.

...

(e) Arrearages and other obligations and liabilities.

(1) Leases of premises. Rent amounts for a lease described in subsection (b)(1) that are unpaid for the period preceding the effective date of the lease termination shall be paid on a prorated bases. The lessor may not impose an early termination charge, but any taxes, summonses, or other obligations and liabilities of the lessee in accordance with the terms of the lease, including reasonable charges to the lessee for excess wear, that are due and unpaid at the time of termination of the lease shall be paid by the lessee.

...

(f) Rent paid in advance. Rents or lease amounts paid in advance for a period after the effective date of the termination of the lease shall be refunded to the lessee by the lessor (or the lessor's assignee or the assignee's agent) within 30 days of the effective date of the termination of the lease.

(g) Relief to lessor. Upon application by the lessor to a court before the termination date provided in the written notice, relief granted by this section to a servicemember may be modified as justice and equity require.

(h) Misdemeanor. Any person who knowingly seizes, holds, or detains the personal effects, security deposit, or other property of a servicemember or a servicemember's dependent who lawfully terminates a lease covered by this section, or who knowingly interferes with the removal of such property from premises covered by such lease, for the purpose of subjecting or attempting to subject any of such property to a claim for rent accruing subsequent to the date of termination of such lease, or attempts to do so, shall be fined as provided in title 18, United States Code, or imprisoned for not more than one year, or both.

(i) Definitions.

    (1) Military orders. The term "military orders," with respect to a servicemember, means official military orders, or any notification, certification, or verification from the servicemember's commanding officer, with respect to the servicemember's current or future military duty status.

...

§ 538. Extension of protections to dependents [Sec. 308]

Upon application to a court, a dependent of a servicemember is entitled to the protections of this title if the dependent's ability to comply with a lease, contract, bailment, or other obligation is materially affected by reason of the servicemember's military service.

Title VIII – Civil Liability

§ 597. Enforcement by the Attorney General [Section 801]

(a) Civil action. The Attorney General may commence a civil action in any appropriate district court of the United States against any person who –

    (1) engages in a pattern or practice of violating this Act [50 U.S.C. App. §§ 501 et seq.]; of

    (2) engages in a violation of this Act that raises an issue of significant public importance.

(b) Relief. In a civil action commenced under subsection (a), the court may –

    (1) grant any appropriate equitable or declaratory relief with respect to the violation of this Act;

    (2) award all other appropriate relief, including monetary damages, to any person aggrieved by the violation; and

    (3) may, to vindicate the public interest, assess a civil penalty –

        (A) in an amount not exceeding $55,000 for a first violation; and

(B) in an amount not exceeding $110,000 for any subsequent violation.

(c) Intervention. Upon timely application, a person aggrieved by a violation of this Act with respect to which the civil action is commenced may intervene in such action, and may obtain such appropriate relief as the person could obtain in a civil action under section 802 [50 U.S.C. App. § 597a] with respect to that violation, along with costs and a reasonable attorney fee.

§ 597a. Private right of action [Section 802]

(a) In general. Any person aggrieved by a violation of this Act [50 U.S.C. App. §§ 501 et seq.] may in a civil action –

(1) obtain any appropriate equitable or declaratory relief with respect to the violation; and

(2) recover all other appropriate relief, including monetary damages.

(b) Costs and attorneys fees. The court may award to a person aggrieved by a violation of this Act who prevails in an action brought under subsection (a) the costs of the action, including a reasonable attorney fee.

§ 597b. Preservation of remedies [Section 803]

Nothing in Section 801 or 802 [50 U.S.C. App. §§ 597 or 597a] shall be construed to preclude or limit any remedy otherwise available under other law, including consequential and punitive damages.

Appendix D

Forms

A number of forms are provided here for the reader's convenience. Use of a particular form is "at your own risk" and *shall not* be deemed advisable or recommended merely by its inclusion in this book. If you have questions whether a particular form, instrument, or other document is appropriate for any given situation, you should consult with a qualified attorney.

- Form letter: demand for possession for nonpayment
- Form letter: demand for possession, reletting as agent
- Form letter: refusal of partial payment
- Form letter: refusal of late payment
- Form letter: termination of lease
- Example: Typical Dispossessory Affidavit (to be filed by landlord)
- Example: Typical Dispossessory Answer (to be filed by tenant)
- Example: Typical Dispossessory Judgment (to be used by court)
- Plaintiff's Post-Judgment Interrogatories to Defendant Pursuant to O.C.G.A. § 15-10-50(d)
- Motion and Order Appointing Special Process Server
- Consent Order [example showing payment arrangement for past-due rent]
- Consent Order [example showing repair-and-deduct order]

Form letter: demand for possession for nonpayment

Re: Lease Agreement dated _ ("Lease") for _ ("Premises")

Dear _,

As of the date of this letter, you owe $_ pursuant to the Lease. This amount includes unpaid rent for the months of _, as well as certain other charges contemplated by the Lease, which the Lease provides is due and payable as additional rent. A statement showing a detailed breakdown of the balance due is enclosed.

Your failure to pay the balance due in a timely manner leaves you in default of the Lease. You may cure that default by delivering payment in full (cash, money order, or certified check only) of the above-stated balance due to me within ten (10) days of your receipt of this letter. If you fail to timely tender payment in full as demanded herein, then I will have no alternative but to pursue the collection of this claim by any appropriate legal means.

In addition, if you fail to timely tender payment in full as demanded herein, you have until 5:00 p.m. on the tenth (10th) day after your receipt of this letter to remove your property from the Premises, vacate the same, and surrender the Premises to me. Demand for possession of the Premises is hereby made. If you fail to timely surrender the Premises as demanded herein, I will commence dispossessory proceedings as provided by Georgia law to have you evicted from the Premises.

As provided by the Lease, no failure by me to exercise any power under the Lease constitutes a waiver of that power, and no failure by me to insist on your strict compliance with the Lease constitutes a waiver of my right to do so. Accordingly, demand is hereby made for payment of rent and other amounts arising under the Lease, as those amounts come due.

Finally, if I am forced to retain the services of an attorney, I will seek recovery of my legal fees and expenses. Pursuant to O.C.G.A. § 13-1-11, you are hereby notified that unless you pay the above-stated balance due within ten (10) days from your receipt of this letter, I will seek the recovery of my attorney's fees and expenses of litigation from you, along with the principal debt you already owe.

Please be guided accordingly.

Form letter: demand for possession, reletting as agent

Re: Lease Agreement dated _ ("Lease") for _ ("Premises")

Dear _,

As of the date of this letter, you owe $_ pursuant to the Lease. This amount includes unpaid rent for the months of _, as well as certain other charges contemplated by the Lease, which the Lease provides is due and payable as additional rent. A statement showing a detailed breakdown of the balance due is enclosed.

Your failure to pay the balance due in a timely manner leaves you in default of the Lease. You may cure that default by delivering payment in full (cash, money order, or certified check only) of the above-stated balance due to me within ten (10) days of your receipt of this letter. If you fail to timely tender payment in full as demanded herein, then I will have no alternative but to pursue the collection of this claim by any appropriate legal means.

As provided by the Lease, no failure by me to exercise any power under the Lease constitutes a waiver of that power, and no failure by me to insist on your strict compliance with the Lease constitutes a waiver of my right to do so. Accordingly, demand is hereby made for payment of rent and other amounts arising under the Lease, as those amounts come due.

If you fail to timely tender payment in full as demanded herein, pursuant to the Lease, without terminating the same and in consideration of your breach of the same, I will re-enter and rent the Premises to another tenant at the best rate I can obtain with reasonable effort, without advertisement and by private negotiations, for any term and on such terms and conditions as I deem proper or appropriate. If there is a deficiency between the rent due under your Lease and the rent due from the new tenant, you will be liable for the same, as provided by the Lease.

Finally, if I am forced to retain the services of an attorney, I will seek recovery of my legal fees and expenses. Pursuant to O.C.G.A. § 13-1-11, you are hereby notified that unless you pay the above-stated balance due within ten (10) days from your receipt of this letter, I will seek the recovery of my attorney's fees and expenses of litigation from you, along with the principal debt you already owe.

Please be guided accordingly.

Form letter: refusal of partial payment

Re: Lease Agreement dated _ ("Lease") for _ ("Premises")

Dear _,

Enclosed please find your check number _ dated _ in the amount of $_, which I received on _. This is a partial payment, however, as your current balance due is $_. As I have not agreed to accept partial payment, your tender of such partial payment is hereby rejected. Demand for possession of the premises is hereby made.

Please be guided accordingly.

Form letter: refusal of late payment

Re: Lease Agreement dated _ ("Lease") for _ ("Premises")

Dear _,

Enclosed please find your check number _ dated _ in the amount of $_, which I received on _. Your tender of such payment is tardy and is hereby rejected. Demand for possession of the premises is hereby made.

Please be guided accordingly.

Form letter: termination of lease

Re: Lease Agreement dated _ ("Lease") for _ ("Premises")
Dear _,

Based on your failure to pay monthly rental for _, and your continued failure to timely cure this default after written notice thereof, you are hereby notified of my decision to terminate the Lease. Pursuant to the Lease, demand for possession is hereby made. You are to immediately vacate the Premises and surrender possession of the same to me.

Please be guided accordingly.

Example: Typical Dispossessory Affidavit
(to be filed by landlord)

<table>
<tr>
<td>

_____

_____

_____

(Plaintiff(s) Name & Address)
Day Phone Number: _____

VS.

_____

_____

_____

(Defendant(s) Name & Address)
Telephone numbers: _____

</td>
<td>

MAGISTRATE COURT OF GWINNETT COUNTY
STATE OF GEORGIA

_____

DISPOSSESSORY PROCEEDING

_____

CASE NO. _____

INFO & FORMS ON THE INTERNET

E-mail: mag@gwinnettcounty.com

</td>
</tr>
</table>

Personally appeared the undersigned affiant who on oath says that affiant is (owner), (attorney at law), (agent) for Plaintiff(s) herein, and that Defendant(s) is/are in possession as tenant of premises at the address as stated above, in Gwinnett County, the property of said Plaintiff(s). Plaintiff(s) attest(s) that there are no other person(s)/entity(ies) or known occupant(s) with whom Plaintiff(s) has/have a landlord tenant relationship. FURTHER THAT: (check applicable claim(s)):

[ ] tenant fails to pay the rent which is now past due;
[ ] tenant holds the premises over and beyond the term for which they were rented or leased to tenant;
[ ] tenant is a tenant at sufferance;
[ ] Other: _____
_____ ; and
THAT Plaintiff(s) is/are entitled to recover any and all rent that may come due until this action is finally concluded. Plaintiff(s) desires and has demanded possession of the premises and Defendant(s) has/have failed and refused to deliver said possession. WHEREFORE, Plaintiff(s) demand(s) (a) possession of the premises; (b) past due rent of $_____; (c) rent accruing up to the date of judgment or vacancy at the rate of

$_____ per day. (Calculate daily rental rate, if seeking rent accruing to date of judgment or vacancy.)

(d) _____
_____

Sworn to and subscribed before me,
this _____ day of _____, 20_____.

_____   _____
                                    Affiant [   ] Owner   [   ] Attorney at Law   [   ] Agent
Magistrate or Deputy Clerk

SUMMONS -- To the Sheriff of Gwinnett County or lawful deputies of the Sheriff -- GREETINGS:
The Defendant(s) is/are commanded and required to file an answer to said affidavit in writing or orally in person at the Magistrate Court of Gwinnett County, Lawrenceville, Georgia on or before the seventh (7th) day after the date of service of this affidavit and summons. If such answer is not made, a Writ of Possession and/or Judgment shall issue as provided by law. Witness the Honorable George Hutchinson, Chief Magistrate of said Court.

This _____ day of _____, 20 _____.
                                    _____
                                    Magistrate or Deputy Clerk

WRIT OF POSSESSION
To the Sheriff of Gwinnett County or lawful deputies of the Sheriff: You are hereby commanded to remove said Defendant(s), and any other person(s)/entities whose presence upon the premises is through the tenancy of Defendant(s) together with Defendant(s)/their property thereon from said premises and to deliver full and quiet possession of the same to the Plaintiff(s) herein effective: 1. (Instanter); or 2. (On _____, 20_____; or, 3. Pursuant to the terms of a consent judgment filed herewith dated _____, 20_____.

This _____ day of _____, 20 _____.
                                    _____
                                    Magistrate

PINK Original; YELLOW & WHITE: Copies   Q:Magforms\forms\MAG 30-02 **Dispossessory** proceeding

113

Example: Typical Dispossessory Answer
(to be filed by tenant)

MAGISTRATE COURT OF GWINNETT COUNTY, GEORGIA

_____
PLAINTIFF(s)

VS

_____
DEFENDANT(s)

CIVIL ACTION FILE NO. _____

(All answers and counterclaims MUST BE FILED WITH THE CLERK within 7 days of the date of service.)

DISPOSSESSORY ANSWER
(Please note and then use another sheet(s) for additional space, as needed.)

_____ I am the Defendant. I am filing an Answer I state the following in response to Plaintiff's claim in this lawsuit:

_____ I do not have a landlord tenant relationship with the plaintiff.

_____ My landlord did not give me the proper notice that my lease or rental agreement was terminated in accordance with the terms of our lease. The landlord did not properly demand that I move before filing the lawsuit.

_____ My landlord terminated my lease without a valid reason.

_____ I do not owe any rent to my landlord.

_____ I offered and had the money to pay my rent on or before the date I usually pay, but my landlord refused to accept it.

_____ My landlord would not accept my rent, correct late fees and the court costs. I had all the money to pay.

_____ My landlord failed to repair the property. This failure has lowered its value or resulted in other damages more than the rent claimed.

_____ I am a residential tenant. This is my first dispossessory action. I am paying all my rent, late fees and court costs to the clerk.

_____ My landlord is not entitled to evict me or secure a money judgment for the following additional reasons: (attach if necessary)

_____

COUNTERCLAIM - (Please note and then use another sheet(s) for additional space, as needed.)

_____ My landlord owes me $_____ for the following reason(s):

_____ My landlord failed to repair my property. Due to this failure, its value has been reduced $_____ each month for _____ months.

_____ Since my landlord failed to make requested repairs, I made these repairs. I made these repairs that cost $_____. I have all my receipts. I will bring the receipts and all documents concerning these payments to my trial.

_____ My landlord's failure to repair resulted in damages of $_____ to my person and/or property.

WHEREFORE, I ask this Court to:
(a)   Dismiss Plaintiff's lawsuit with all costs assessed against Plaintiff.
(b)   Enter a judgment in my favor and against Plaintiff; and
(c)   Grant such other and further relief as the Court deems just and proper.

_____   _____
(Print name of Defendant filing answer & address)   Signature of Defendant filing answer/ Attorney

_____   Bar # _____

EACH DEFENDANT MUST FILE THEIR OWN ANSWER. Attorneys may file answers for more than one defendant, pro se litigants cannot.

Commercial LL – A– L, 9:00 AM, 1C Or Plaintiffs who use a filing service	Commercial LL – M - Z, 9:00 AM, 1D Or Plaintiffs who use a filing service	All other LL's, 1:00 PM, 1D

NOTICE OF TRIAL DATE

The Plaintiff(s) and Defendant(s) are required to appear for trial in Courtroom _____ on the _____ day of _____,

20_____ at _____ o'clock _____. M. Courtroom 1 _____, Gwinnett Justice & Administration Building, 75 Langley Drive, Lawrenceville, GA. 30045-6900. If you have an attorney, please notify your attorney to be present with you.

This _____day of _____, 20_____.

_____   _____
DEFENDANT   DEPUTY CLERK

114

Example: Typical Dispossessory Judgment
(to be used by court)

_____

_____
                    Plaintiff(s)
vs.

_____

_____
                    Defendant(s)

**MAGISTRATE COURT OF GWINNETT COUNTY
STATE OF GEORGIA**

DISPOSSESSORY JUDGMENT

CASE NO. _____

[ ] JUDGMENT   [ ] CONSENT JUDGMENT   [ ] DEFAULT JUDGMENT   [ ] DISMISSAL
The above case having come on regularly to be heard, the Court makes the following findings: (check only if applicable)

[ ] Defensive pleadings filed by Defendant(s)
[ ] Counterclaim filed by Defendant(s)
[ ] Plaintiff(s) appeared   [ ] Plaintiff(s) failed to appear
[ ] Defendant(s) appeared   [ ] Defendant(s) failed to appear

[ ]Voluntary dismissal w/out prejudice - Statement of Claim *(may be refiled)*
[ ] Voluntary dismissal - Counterclaim
[ ] Stipulated settlement and dismissal   [ ] Court Dismissal
[ ] Contested hearing held

WRIT OF POSSESSION: IT IS HEREBY **ORDERED** and **ADJUDGED** that a WRIT OF POSSESSION **(shall) (shall not)** be issued:

a. **[ ]** Instanter

b. **[ ]** on_____

c. **[ ]** Upon written affidavit to this court of defendant's failure to pay plaintiff(s) $_____ principal, $_____ interest,

    $_____ attorney fees, and $_____ court costs:

    (1) on or before _____ , _____

    (2) as follows: _____

_____

MONEY JUDGMENT: **[ ]** Is not authorized, **[ ]** no personal service; **[ ]** tenant at sufferance; **[ ]** other _____.
Or, is set forth below as the net judgment, for all claim(s) and counterclaim(s) filed with the court, without having been dismissed:

d. **[ ]** Judgment is entered in favor of the defendant(s) against plaintiff(s).

e. **[ ]** Plaintiff(s) recover judgment against defendant(s) _____ in the sum of

    $_____ principal, of which **[ ]** all; or $_____ ; is past due rent, $_____ interest,

    $_____ attorney fees, and $_____ court costs, and interest at _____ % per annum as shall accrue hereafter.

f. **[ ]** Plaintiff(s) has/have Consent Judgment against defendant(s) _____ for the sum of

    $_____ principal, $_____ interest, $_____ attorney fees, and $_____ court costs as follows:

_____

No FiFa will issue and no garnishment or other action will be taken on said consent judgment as long as payments are timely paid, as ordered. If the defendant(s) fail to make payment or should payment be made more than 5 days beyond the due date, the Clerk of Magistrate Court shall issue a FiFa in the amount then outstanding upon written notice from the plaintiff(s) that payments have not been made as agreed and upon payment of the applicable FiFa fee.

g. **[ ]** Plaintiff(s) shall be paid $_____ ; or, **[ ]** defendant(s) shall be paid $_____ ; now being held in the court registry.

h. **[ ]** Defendant(s) recover judgment against plaintiff(s) _____ in the amount of

    $_____ principal, $_____ interest, and $_____ attorney fees.

i. **[ ]** Defendant(s) counterclaim is hereby denied (in its entirety) (as to the issue of_____)

j. **[ ]** In the event of an appeal, pursuant to O.C.G.A. 44-7-56, in order for the defendant(s) to remain in possession of the premises, the defendant(s) shall immediately pay into the registry of the court the sum of $_____ as past due rent through today's date. The defendant(s) shall immediately

pay future rent of $_____for the balance of rent owed for this month, and then the amount of $_____ / month beginning on _____ and continuing on the same day of each month thereafter until the issue has been finally determined upon appeal. The failure to comply with this provision may cause an immediate writ of possession for possession of the premises to be issued instanter by a court of competent jurisdiction.

Duties of ALL judgment creditors: Upon payment of the entire debt upon which a judgment or FiFa has been issued, the judgment creditor shall, in writing, timely (within 60 days) direct the clerk(s) of the appropriate court(s) to: (1) cancel the writ of FiFa, if a writ was issued; (2) mark the judgment satisfied. Failure to timely comply may subject the judgment creditor to monetary damages, O.C.G.A. § 9-13-80.

This _____ day of _____ , 20_____.

CONSENTED TO BY:

_____

_____

_____
                    Magistrate

Q:\Magforms\Forms\Dispossessory Judgment Mag. 30-04

115

IN THE MAGISTRATE COURT OF _____ COUNTY
STATE OF GEORGIA

_____ ,)
       Plaintiff,   )   CIVIL ACTION FILE
v.   )   NO. _____
_____ ,)
       Defendant.   )

PLAINTIFF'S POST-JUDGMENT INTERROGATORIES TO DEFENDANT PURSUANT TO O.C.G.A. § 15-10-50(d)

The Plaintiff in the above-styled action requests that you answer the following interrogatories separately, fully, and under oath and serve such answers on said Plaintiff at Plaintiff's address shown above by mail or hand delivery within thirty (30) days after the service of these interrogatories.

Space has been provided for you to clearly and legibly write your answers directly underneath each interrogatory. You are not required to answer in this fashion, but if you do, you are advised to retain a copy of these interrogatories and your answers thereto for your records. If your answer to any particular interrogatory requires more space than allotted here, then attach additional sheets as necessary.

1. List your full name, home phone number, and address, including apartment number and ZIP Code.

2. List the name, address, and phone number of your employer(s).

3. Describe and state the location of each piece of real estate in which you own any interest.

4. Give the name, address, phone number, and a description of the nature of any business venture in which you own any interest.

5. List the names, addresses, and phone numbers of all persons who owe money to you and specify the amounts owed.

6. List the names and addresses of all banks or savings institutions where you have any sums of money deposited and

identify the accounts by number.

7.   List and give the present location of all items of personal property owned by you that have a value of more than $100.00.

NOTICE

YOU ARE REQUIRED TO PROVIDE COMPLETE ANSWERS TO THE ABOVE-STATED QUESTIONS TO THE PLAINTIFF WITHIN THIRTY (30) DAYS AFTER SERVICE OF THESE INTER-ROGATORIES UPON YOU. IF YOU DO NOT ANSWER, OR DO NOT ANSWER COMPLETELY, YOU MAY BECOME SUBJECT TO THE SANCTIONS PROVIDED BY LAW FOR CONTEMPT OF COURT. IF YOU NEED FURTHER INSTRUCTION OR IF YOU NEED ASSISTANCE IN ANSWERING THE QUESTIONS CONTACT THE COURT AT ONCE.

NOTICE OF FILING ORIGINAL DISCOVERY REQUESTS

Defendant is hereby notified that Plaintiff has caused the original of these Interrogatories to be filed with the Office of the Clerk of Court.

CERTIFICATE OF SERVICE

I have served the Defendant at the address noted in the style of this pleading with a copy of these Interrogatories via statutory overnight delivery on the date written below.

Respectfully submitted this, the ___ day of _____, 20___

_____
(signature)

_____
(print name)

(notice to defendant on next page)

NOTICE: YOUR ANSWERS TO PLAINTIFF'S INTERROGATO-RIES MUST BE VERIFIED USING THIS FORM OR ONE WHICH IS SUBSTANTIALLY SIMILAR, WHICH YOU MUST SIGN BE-FORE A NOTARY PUBLIC OR OTHER ATTESTING OFFICIAL. PLEASE NOTE YOU ARE REQUIRED TO VERIFY YOUR RE-SPONSES IN WRITING WHETHER YOU CHOOSE TO ANSWER THEM BY WRITING ON A COPY OF THE INTERROGATORIES THEMSELVES OR WHETHER YOU CHOOSE TO ANSWER THEM IN SOME OTHER WRITTEN FORM.

VERIFICATION

STATE OF GEORGIA
COUNTY OF _____

I, _____, being first duly sworn on oath, state the foregoing are true and complete answers to the Interrogatories propounded by Plaintiff to Defendant.

_____
(signature)

Sworn to and subscribed before me
this _____ day of _____, 20_____.

_____
Notary Public

[SEAL]

IN THE STATE COURT OF _____ COUNTY
STATE OF GEORGIA

_____,	)
Plaintiff,	) CIVIL ACTION FILE
v.	) NO. _____
_____,	)
Defendant.	)

PLAINTIFF'S MOTION FOR APPOINTMENT OF SPECIAL PROCESS SERVER

Comes now the Plaintiff herein, by and through counsel, and pursuant to O.C.G.A. § 9-11-4(c) and shows this Court that expedited service on the Defendant is necessary and requests the appointment of a special process server to serve Defendant, as authorized under the law.

WHEREFORE, Plaintiff moves this Court for an Order appointing an agent of _____, who is not an interested party to the suit, is a citizen of the United States and is 18 years of age or over, to serve Defendant with the Dispossessory Proceeding, and to make a return on that service pursuant to O.C.G.A. § 9-11-4(c).

Respectfully submitted this, the ____ day of _____, 20____

_____
(signature)

_____
(print name)

(proposed order on next page)

IN THE STATE COURT OF _____ COUNTY
STATE OF GEORGIA

_____)
      Plaintiff,   )   CIVIL ACTION FILE
v.   )   NO. _____
_____)
      Defendant.   )

ORDER APPOINTING SPECIAL PROCESS SERVER

Upon Motion of the Plaintiff for Appointment of Special Process Server, and it appearing appropriate, just and equitable,

IT IS CONSIDERED, ORDERED AND ADJUDGED that an agent of _____ is a citizen of the United States, is 18 years of age or over, and is a party having no interest in the above-styled case, and is hereby appointed special agent for service of a Dispossessory Proceeding in this case upon the Defendant.

SO ORDERED this, the _____ day of _____, 20_____.

_____
Judge, State Court of _____ County

120

IN THE MAGISTRATE COURT OF _____ COUNTY
STATE OF GEORGIA

_____,)	
Plaintiff,)	CIVIL ACTION FILE
v.)	NO. _____
_____,)	
Defendant.)	

CONSENT ORDER
[example showing payment arrangement for past-due rent]

WHEREAS, Plaintiff ("Landlord") has asserted a claim against Defendant ("Tenant") for unpaid and past due rent for the months of _, in the total principal amount of $_; and

WHEREAS, the parties acknowledge and agree the total due as of _, is $_ (the "Balance Due"), which amount Tenant acknowledges and agrees it owes Landlord as of that date; and

WHEREAS, the Parties have agreed to a payment schedule to retire the Balance Due, as provided herein;

NOW THEREFORE, the Parties have agreed, and the Court hereby ORDERS, as follows:

1.

Tenant will pay $_.00 per month, with the first payment due on _, and successive payments due no later than the first day of each subsequent month until the Balance Due is paid in full. Assuming Tenant timely makes the payments required in this Paragraph, Landlord will stay any further efforts to collect the Balance Due. Upon timely receipt of each and every payment required by this Paragraph, Landlord will waive any additional claims for interest, attorney's fees, or other sums claimed due that arise from the debt resulting in the Balance Due.

2.

In the event of a missed payment, Tenant shall be considered in default of this Consent Order, in which event Landlord shall be entitled, at its sole option, to obtain a Writ of Possession, Money Judgment, and issuance of a Writ of Fieri Facias ("Judgment") against Tenant for the principal balance outstanding, less all payments received. Landlord shall obtain its Judgment in the above-styled civil action by submitting to the Clerk of this Court its (or its attorney's) affidavit certifying the past-due outstanding balance.

3.

Tenant hereby waives and/or dismisses any and all claims which it has asserted or may assert against Landlord with prejudice. When the Balance Due and any additional interest or attorney's fees are paid in full, Landlord shall dismiss its remaining claims against Tenant with prejudice.

4.

Time is of the essence of this Consent Order.
SO ORDERED this, the _____ day of _____, 20_____.

_____
Judge, Magistrate Court of _____ County

Agreed by Plaintiff/Landlord:
_____

Agreed by Defendant/Tenant:
_____

IN THE MAGISTRATE COURT OF _____ COUNTY
STATE OF GEORGIA

_____,)
     Plaintiff,   )   CIVIL ACTION FILE
v.   )   NO. _____
_____,)
     Defendant.   )

CONSENT ORDER
[example showing repair-and-deduct order]

WHEREAS, Plaintiff ("Landlord") has asserted a claim against Defendant ("Tenant") for unpaid and past due rent for the months of _, in the total principal amount of $_ (the "Unpaid Rent"), which Tenant acknowledges and agrees has not been paid; and

WHEREAS, Tenant has asserted a counterclaim against Landlord alleging that Landlord has failed to make certain repairs; and

WHEREAS, the Parties have agreed to attempt to resolve their claims against one another, as provided herein;

NOW THEREFORE, the Parties have agreed, and the Court hereby ORDERS, as follows:

1.

Tenant will pay the Unpaid Rent into the Registry of the Court by _, and will continue to pay $_.00 per month into the Registry of the Court as rent accruing during the pendency of this case, with the first such payment due on _, and successive payments due no later than the first day of each subsequent month.

2.

Landlord will perform the following repairs within _ days of this Consent Order: _. Tenant agrees to allow Landlord such access to the rented premises as is reasonably necessary to make the repairs required herein, at such times as are reasonable.

3.

This case is reset for _ at _ in courtroom _ of the _ County Courthouse. The Parties are ordered to appear at that time and to report to the Court whether the repairs detailed above have been made and the funds due from the Tenant have been paid. The Court shall determine at that time the final disposition of the funds then held in the Registry of the Court.

4.

Time is of the essence of this Consent Order.

SO ORDERED this, the _____ day of _____, 20_____.

_____

Judge, Magistrate Court of _____ County

Agreed by Plaintiff/Landlord:

_____

Agreed by Defendant/Tenant:

_____

Appendix E

Practice Pointers

> **Practice Pointer #1:** If possible, the landlord should be sure to include a provision in the lease agreement allowing him to reenter the premises upon abandonment for the purpose of reletting the same as the agent for the abandoning tenant, as well as for the purpose of securing and protecting the premises.

> **Practice Pointer #2:** If there is any doubt, the landlord should follow the dispossessory process.

> **Practice Pointer #3:** Generally speaking, the landlord should file and prosecute dispossessory actions in Magistrate Court, where the case will generally move more quickly and and cheaply.

> **Practice Pointer #4:** The landlord should generally only consider filing a distraint proceeding if the tenant has abandoned property of significant value on the premises under circumstances where the landlord has an independent right to enter and secure the premises.

Practice Pointer #5: The landlord should consider methods of delivering the written demand for possession other than regular or certified mail, to ensure he can prove delivery of the demand for possession later.

Practice Pointer #6: The landlord should always make a written demand for possession, and he should thereafter behave as if he wants the tenant to vacate the premises.

Practice Pointer #7: The landlord who wishes to evict a tenant for failing to pay rent must not accept rent payments in any amount after making a demand for possession.

Practice Pointer #8: The landlord should attach copies of the lease agreement, demand for possession, and any other relevant documents as exhibits to the initial affidavit.

Practice Pointer #9: The landlord should use the court's own form whenever possible.

Practice Pointer #10: If the landlord wishes to recover a money judgment against the tenant, the landlord must ensure the tenant is personally served with process in the dispossessory action, and the landlord should consider using a specially appointed process server, if appropriate.

Practice Pointer #11: The landlord should obtain and serve subpoenas on each of his trial witnesses, even if they are "friendly" witnesses.

Practice Pointer #12: If the landlord has refused an attempted tender of rent by the tenant, the landlord should write a follow-up letter or other communication memorializing that refusal and the reasons therefor, and copies of that communication should be available to be used as an exhibit at trial.

Practice Pointer #13: If the landlord desires a money judgment for any reason, and the total amount requested must be calculated somehow, the landlord should prepare a written summary of those calculations and be prepared to admit that written summary as an exhibit at trial.

Practice Pointer #14: The landlord should share all of his trial exhibits with the tenant at his earliest opportunity, to save time at trial.

Practice Pointer #15: The landlord should be prepared to tactfully remind the court that if the trial must be continued to a date more than two weeks after the tenant was served with the landlord's affidavit, the court must require the payment of rent into the court's registry.

Practice Pointer #16: The landlord who successfully obtains a money judgment against the tenant should ask the court to order that a writ of fieri facias should be issued immediately.

Practice Pointer #17: The landlord should have kept a copy of at least one check from the tenant, to give him a possible avenue of garnishment.

Practice Pointer #18: The landlord should not apply any portion of the security deposit paid by the tenant to past-due rent unless the lease agreement specifically allows him to do so.

Practice Pointer #19: The landlord should always ask the trial court to include a provision in the judgment requiring the tenant to continue to pay rent into the Court Registry as a condition of maintaining an appeal.

Practice Pointer #20: The landlord should try to ensure all evidence introduced at trial in the Magistrate Court is somehow filed into that court's file, by filing a post-trial affidavit with exhibits attached, if necessary.

Practice Pointer #21: The landlord should investigate how long it will take to have the writ of possession executed by the county sheriff or marshal, and he should consider hiring an eviction servicing company if appropriate.

Practice Pointer #22: The prudent landlord will attempt mediation if possible and will keep an open mind throughout the mediation process, even if it seems obvious the case will not settle.

Practice Pointer #23: Counsel for the landlord should consider using mediation to give a *pro se* tenant his proverbial "day in court."

Appendix F

Quiet Enjoyment and the Obligation to Maintain

As was explained at the end of Chapter 3, a "covenant of quiet enjoyment" is implied in every lease agreement, even those which are not in writing. Simply put, the landlord has a duty to provide the premises to the tenant and cannot interfere with the tenant's enjoyment of those premises, even if the tenant fails to pay rent or otherwise breaches the agreement. Of course, if the tenant does breach the lease, the law provides for the tenant to be evicted, which is what this book is all about.

A breach of the covenant of quiet enjoyment has to be pretty severe to be actionable. However, that does not mean the landlord can get away with failing to properly maintain the premises in good repair. This Appendix explains the parties obligations relating to maintenance and repair in greater detail.

Maintenance and Repair. Landlord liability under Georgia law essentially boils down to one basic, time-honored concept – foreseeability. If a landlord is aware of a problem and has a reasonable opportunity to remedy the same, then the landlord must make reasonable effort to do so, or else face potential liability for injuries or damages suffered as a result of the failure to resolve the problem.

For example, the landlord is generally required to keep the rented premises in good repair, and the landlord's failure in this regard will give the tenant a right to claim damages.[51] In Georgia, any provision in a residential lease agreement which attempts to shift liability for repairs to the tenant is void and unenforceable as a matter of law.[52] In addition, any provision in a lease agreement which purports to exculpate the landlord from any liability or responsibility arising from its own negligence is invalid and unenforceable, whether the lease is residential or commercial.[53]

Similarly, a landlord is required to deliver possession of the rented premises to the tenant free from latent defects, that is, a defect which is hidden or is otherwise not immediately obvious. A landlord impliedly warrants rented premises are in good repair when they are rented. If they are not in good repair, by reason of a latent defect, the landlord is liable if he actually knew of the defect, or if by the exercise of ordinary care he could have discovered the defect, if the latent defect is the proximate cause of the injury.[54]

A patent defect existing at the time possession is delivered to the tenant, however, does not create liability in the landlord. If the tenant knows about the defect (or reasonably should know) before taking possession, and takes possession anyway, he assumes the risks associated with the defect, and the landlord is not liable.[55]

As for repair issues that arise after the tenant has taken possession, the key is usually notice. The tenant is generally under a duty to bring the need for repairs to the landlord's attention, and the landlord cannot be liable for a failure to repair unless and until he is notified of the repair issue and given a reasonable opportunity to remedy the same.[56] The landlord is under no independent duty to inspect the premises while the tenant occupies them,[57] and indeed, unless the lease agreement provides to the contrary, the landlord may not even have the right to enter the premises to perform such an inspection.[58] However, once the landlord is put on proper notice, he has a duty to inspect the condition for himself and to complete proper repairs within a reasonable time.[59] This includes repairing latent defects which the landlord should reasonably be expected to discover upon an inspection of a patent defect that is brought to the landlord's attention.[60]

Tenant Remedies. A tenant who has notified his landlord of a repair issue has three potential avenues of relief if the landlord does not address the issue within a reasonable timeframe. The first, and probably most commonly employed, is colloquially known as "repair and deduct" – basically, the tenant performs or pays for the repairs himself, and deducts the costs paid by him from future rent payments as they come due. The prudent tenant will provide the landlord with as much written notice as possible and would be well-advised to obtain written estimates from more than one contractor before causing the repairs to be performed. Although there is no requirement that the tenant use identical materials, the tenant should be reasonable and is not entitled to perform substantial upgrades or use significantly superior materials to what existed before. Assuming the tenant gives the landlord plenty of notice of what he intends to do before he does it, the tenant will likely survive a future suit alleging he has failed to pay his rent.

Alternatively, the tenant may file suit for damages under a traditional breach of contract theory. This may be preferable if the tenant's damages substantially exceed the cost of the repair. This is more likely to arise in a commercial lease, and one should be mindful that commercial leases are typically far more detailed than residential leases regarding repair and maintenance issues. Specifically, the commercial tenant should be sure the lease does not contractually shift responsibility for such issues from the landlord to the tenant; as noted above, such a contractual provision would be unenforceable in a residential lease by statute, but there is no such statutory prohibition in place for commercial leases.

The law is clear that the tenant is not allowed to withhold payment of rent in the face of a persistent repair failure. However, the tenant will often (and perhaps understandably) do exactly that. If the landlord then sues for rent, the tenant will be presented with a third alternative, which is recoupment in a suit for rent. Essentially, this will boil down to an offset in damages of the costs and damages suffered by the tenant against the unpaid rent due to the landlord. This is generally not a recommended alternative from the tenant's perspective, since the breach of his obligation to pay rent can cost him the right to retain possession of the rented premises, even if he is entitled to relief because of the repair failure.

Other Maintenance/Repair Issues. Georgia law regarding the duty of the landlord to provide security for its tenants is consistent with the "foreseeability" concept noted above. The landlord is not ordinarily charged with ensuring the tenant's safety, but he does have a duty to exercise ordinary care to prevent something like a third-party criminal attack upon the tenant. However, the tenant may not recover if it can be demonstrated that the tenant has equal or superior knowledge of the risk and fails to exercise ordinary care to protect his own safety.[61] Moreover, the Georgia Court of Appeals has explicitly held that the duty to provide security is not part of the landlord's statutory duty to maintain or repair the premises.[62] If the landlord voluntarily assumes that duty, however, then the landlord can be liable for negligence in failing to carry out that duty.

There is not much case law specific to issues such as mold or carbon monoxide poisoning, but the case law that does exist reaches results one would predict by applying the general principles outlined above. For example, in one case, the tenant filed suit for damages arising from carbon monoxide poisoning that she suffered due to a temporary repair to the roof of the apartment building by the landlord following a tornado.[63] Since there was some evidence that the repair was negligently done, the Georgia Court of Appeals reversed the grant of summary judgment in favor of the landlord. The fact the repair was done by an independent contractor, rather than an employee of the landlord, was irrelevant. Moreover, the fact that the repair was of a temporary nature (a tarp stretched over the roof blocked some vents – a problem that would have been resolved when the permanent roof repair was done and the tarp was removed) was also irrelevant to the Court's analysis.

Conclusions and Practical Implications. There are four practical implications of the above. First, a landlord should always thoroughly inspect his property before delivering possession to a tenant, and ideally a written inspection disclosing all patent defects should be delivered to and signed by the tenant at that time.[64] Second, the lease should carefully explain to the tenant what, specifically, is not covered as a "repair" (e.g., security issues), to help avoid a future argument that the landlord has somehow voluntarily assumed a duty not otherwise ordinarily includable under the generic "duty to maintain". Third, the lease should carefully explain what constitutes adequate notice of a maintenance/repair issue, and that compliance with that provision is required even if notice is given by some other means. Finally, the landlord should be guided, first and foremost, by common sense. If a tenant brings a repair or maintenance issue to the landlord's attention, the landlord should act with reasonable diligence and promptness to repair or otherwise resolve that issue. Failing to do so is simply inviting litigation or other problems down the road.

---

[51] O.C.G.A. §§ 44-7-13, -14.

[52] O.C.G.A. § 44-7-2(b)(1). Note this Code Section only applies in a residential context, and the parties may freely agree to shift the burden of repairing and maintaining the property to the tenant in a commercial lease agreement. Groutas v. McCoy, 219 Ga. App. 252 (1995).

[53] Country Club Apartments, Inc. v. Scott, 154 Ga. App. 217, 219-20 (1980) (residential lease); and Central Warehouse and Development Corp. v. Nostalgia, Inc., 210 Ga. App. 15, 16 (1993) (commercial lease).

[54] Country Club Apts. v. Scott, 154 Ga. App. 217, 219(2) (1980), aff'd 246 Ga. 443 (1980).

[55] Commerce Properties, Inc. v. Linthicum, 209 Ga. App. 853 (1993).

[56] Me Yere v. Withers, 15 Ga. App. 688 (1915).

[57] Davis v. Smith, 169 Ga. App. 635 (1984).

[58] Livaditis v. American Cas. Co. of Reading, Pa., 117 Ga. App. 297 (1968).

[59] Garner v. La Marr, 88 Ga. App. 364 (1953).

[60] Aycock v. Houser, 96 Ga. App. 99 (1957).

[61] Jackson v. Post Properties, Inc., 236 Ga. App. 701 (1999).

[62] Cooperwood v. Auld, 175 Ga. App. 694 (1985).

[63] Atkins v. MRP Park Lake, L.P., 301 Ga. App. 275 (2009).

[64] This is required if the tenant will be paying a security deposit. O.C.G.A. § 44-7-33(a).

Appendix G

Security Deposits

Landlords have a number of strict requirements for handling security deposits. First and foremost, if the landlord (together with his spouse and his minor children) owns more than ten (10) rental units, is an entity rather than a natural person, or uses a property manager, security deposits must be held in escrow.[65] Second, the landlord must present the tenant with a "comprehensive list of any existing damage to the premises," which the tenant must sign, or to which the tenant must provide a written objection.[66] Third, within three (3) business days after the tenant vacates, the landlord must inspect the premises and provide a list of damages to the tenant, who then has five (5) business days to verify the accuracy of the list, or to provide a written objection to the same.[67] Fourth, within one month after termination of the lease or the tenant's occupancy (whichever occurs later), the landlord must return the security deposit, in whole or in part, and if the landlord elects to retain any portion of the security deposit, he must also provide a written statement to the tenant detailing the exact reasons for the retention of that portion.[68]

If the landlord timely follows these requirements, the tenant will lose his right to claim the security deposit retained by the landlord should be returned.[69] If the landlord does not follow these requirements, the landlord loses his right to retain any portion of the security deposit or to bring an action against the tenant for damage to the premises.[70] Moreover, if a landlord is found to have wrongfully withheld any portion of a security deposit, the landlord will be liable for at least the amount wrongfully withheld, and if the landlord cannot demonstrate the wrongful withholding was due to a "bona fide error," the landlord's liability will increase to three times the sum wrongfully withheld, plus reasonable attorney's fees.[71]

Note that the landlord is allowed to retain the security deposit for sums due from the tenant other than for damage to the premises – for example, unpaid rent or other damages caused by the tenant's breach.[72] It is recommended that the lease agreement explicitly notify the tenant that the landlord will be entitled to apply the security deposit to cover these unpaid costs and damages.

---

[65] O.C.G.A. § 44-7-36.

[66] O.C.G.A. § 44-7-33(a).

[67] O.C.G.A. § 44-7-33(b).

[68] O.C.G.A. § 44-7-34(a).

[69] O.C.G.A. § 44-7-33(c).

[70] O.C.G.A. § 44-7-35(a), (b).

[71] O.C.G.A. § 44-7-35(c).

[72] O.C.G.A. § 44-7-34(a).

Glossary

The following is a brief glossary explaining some of the legal words and phrases used in this book in layman's terms. This glossary is *not* intended to be exhaustive. For words and phrases not defined here, or for more technical explanations of terms which are defined here, this author recommends the reader consult an authoritative legal dictionary such as the most current edition of *Black's Law Dictionary*.

- *de novo* **trial or trial** *de novo* - a second trial of a case, usually a retrial on appeal by a court sitting in an appellate capacity, where nothing that happened in any earlier trial is considered in the course of the retrial

- **dispossessory proceeding** - a lawsuit filed by a landlord against his tenant, the object of which is to give the landlord the legal right to possess the rented premises in the form of a writ of possession; a writ of possession is necessary for an eviction to take place

- **distraint proceeding** - a lawsuit filed by a landlord to enforce a lien upon the personal property of his tenant which is located within or upon the rented premises

- **distress proceeding** - synonym for distraint proceeding

- **eviction** - the act of forcibly removing someone from real property; a legal eviction requires the issuance of a valid writ of possession first

- *fieri facias*, **writ of** - see writ of *fieri facias*

- **holding over** - continuing to occupy rented premises after the expiration of a lease agreement
- **landlord** - a person with authority to allow another to occupy real property; typically, the landlord is the owner of the rented premises
- **latent defect** - a defect which is hidden or is otherwise not immediately obvious
- **lessee** - synonym for tenant
- **lessor** - synonym for landlord
- **patent defect** - a defect which is obvious or observable upon a reasonable inspection
- **possession, writ of** - see writ of possession
- *pro se* - representing oneself, that is, proceeding without the assistance of an attorney
- **registry** - an escrow account held by the clerk of court, used for holding funds paid by one party which are at issue in a lawsuit; funds are then disbursed pursuant to a court order, usually to one of the parties
- **relet** - to lease previously rented premises to another tenant
- **tenant** - a person occupying real property which he does not own
- **tenant at sufferance** - a tenant who previously occupied rented premises pursuant to a lease agreement, but who continues to occupy the rented premises after that lease agreement has expired, perhaps without the permission of the landlord
- **tenant at will** - a tenant whose tenancy has no specified time of termination
- **tort** - an injury to one person caused by another person, who is legally responsible to the injured party for the injury; an intentional tort is a tort that was done deliberately, and for which punitive (as opposed to merely consequential) damages may be available

- **writ of *fieri facias*** - (a/k/a "fi.fa."; pronounced "FIGH-fay") a court-issued instrument which constitutes evidence of a money judgment in a form suitable for recording in the general execution docket of a particular jurisdiction (in Georgia, each county has its own general execution docket)
- **writ of possession** - a court order giving a person (typically the landlord) the legal right to possess and occupy real property

Dispossessory Checklist

1. Demand for Possession
   - ○ should be written
   - ○ should be able to prove delivery – use courier or special delivery service

2. File Dispossessory Action
   - ○ use court's form, if available
   - ○ allege one or more of three statutory grounds
     - ❏ tenant is holding over
     - ❏ tenant has failed to pay rent
     - ❏ tenant at sufferance or tenant at will
   - ○ attach as many exhibits as possible, for example:
     - ❏ lease
     - ❏ demand for possession
     - ❏ other correspondence, and proof of delivery

3. Service of Process
   - ○ sheriff or marshal will attempt service at rented premises and will perfect "nail-and-mail" service
   - ○ must have personal service if money judgment sought – consider private process server if necessary

4. Trial
   - ○ bring copies of whatever evidence is needed, for example:
     - ❏ exhibits to dispossessory affidavit
     - ❏ pictures
     - ❏ ledger of payments
     - ❏ summary of damages sought
   - ○ bring witnesses to testify – consider subpoenas
   - ○ mediation may be required first

5. Judgment
   - ○ writ of possession is key
   - ○ money judgment, but only if personal service is perfected
   - ○ ask court to include provision requiring rent to be paid into court registry in the event of an appeal

6. Execute Writ of Possession
   - ○ must schedule with sheriff or marshal
   - ○ must provide own labor to clear property out of rented premises
   - ○ consider bringing locksmith to change locks immediately
   - ○ consider hiring servicing company
     - ❏ servicing company coordinates all of the above
     - ❏ servicing company can sometimes accelerate timing